Bret Harte

A Ward of the Golden Gate

Bret Harte

A Ward of the Golden Gate

ISBN/EAN: 9783743312647

Manufactured in Europe, USA, Canada, Australia, Japa

Cover: Foto ©ninafisch / pixelio.de

Manufactured and distributed by brebook publishing software (www.brebook.com)

Bret Harte

A Ward of the Golden Gate

Bret Harte

A Ward of the Golden Gate

A WARD

OF

THE GOLDEN GATE

BY

BRET HARTE

WITH 59 ILLUSTRATIONS BY STANLEY WOOD

London
CHATTO & WINDUS, PICCADILLY
1890

PRINTED BY
SPOTTISWOODE AND CO., NEW-STREET SQUARE
LONDON

LIST OF ILLUSTRATIONS

'YOU THINK YOU HAVE SAVED HER FROM DISGRACE'—*Frontispiece*

	PAGE
SHE HALTED BEFORE A DOOR MARKED 'MAYOR'S OFFICE'	4
FOR SOME MINUTES THERE WAS ONLY THE RAPID SCRATCHING OF THE MAYOR'S PEN	15
'DO YOU KNOW WHO THAT WOMAN IS?'	21
'I DIDN'T ALLOW YOU'LD REMEMBER ME'	26
TENDED TO INCREASE THEIR GOOD HUMOUR	35
'DE KERNEL WON'T HAVE ANY BUT THE BEST CHAMPAGNE'.	47
PENDLETON PLACED THE PACKET IN HIS VISITOR'S HAND	61
HE MET PAUL'S SMILING FACE IN THE GLASS	64
'TAKE THIS,' HE SAID	68
'GEORGE, DON'T LIE TO ME, OR——'	70
TOOK FROM IT A STRIPED COTTON HANDKERCHIEF.	72
TWO YOUNG GIRLS IN LIGHT SUMMER DRESSES	75
THE THREE GENTLEMEN LIFTED THEIR HATS.	84
'I SUPPOSE IT IS ALL RIGHT,' SHE SAID	92
HE SHARPLY CLOSED THE WINDOW.	113
A CARD IN A SCHOOLGIRL'S HAND	120
HE WAS ENDEAVOURING TO PICK A QUARREL WITH A MAN MERELY ON SUSPICION	132
HE LINGERED ON THE VERANDAH WITH A CIGAR	137
'I HOPE YOU HAVE HAD NO MORE WORDS WITH DON CÆSAR'	144
A PRINTER'S PROOF-SLIP, WHICH HE HURRIEDLY GLANCED OVER.	148

LIST OF ILLUSTRATIONS

	PAGE
'YO GOT ME DAH, SAH! YO GOT ME, DAH!'	162
GEORGE AT ONCE BECAME COMMUNICATIVE	163
HE WAS DRESSED IN A TIGHTLY-BUTTONED BLUE FROCK-COAT	165
THE COLONEL POURED OUT A GLASS OF WHISKY	168
HALTED A MOMENT AT THE DOORWAY	181
A CAVALRYMAN WALKING WITH CLÄRCHEN	182
HIS UNAFFECTED AND SIMPLE GREETING	184
THEY TURNED AWAY TOGETHER	192
CROSSED HER KNEES WITH HER HANDS CLASPED OVER THEM	212
BOTH RODE WELL AND NATURALLY	216
TYING THEIR HORSES TO TWO BUSHES	223
THEIR ELBOWS RESTED UPON THE BROKEN WALL	225
'SO I HEAR YOU, TOO, ARE A CONQUEST OF THE BEAUTIFUL SOUTH AMERICAN'	231
'THAT WILL DO, MR. HATHAWAY; I KNOW ALL'.	250
PREPARED TO FOLLOW THEM	253
HE INFORMED THE PORTER THAT, OWING TO A CALL OF BUSINESS, HE SHOULD TRY AND CATCH THE EXPRESS	255
IT WAS A LADY'S HANDKERCHIEF	259
SHE WAS REGULAR AND RESOLUTE IN FEATURES	263
HE DESCENDED THE STEPS	267
'KATE HOWARD—BY THE ETERNAL!'	269
HOW SOON DID HE THINK THE PATIENT COULD BE REMOVED	277
IT WAS FROM MILLY WOODS	281
SHE RAN QUICKLY TOWARDS HIM	284
MR. WOODS, CALIFORNIAN AND REMINISCENT	293
'SHE FRIGHTENS ME!' SAID YERBA	298
ON HER KNEES BESIDE THE BED	300

A WARD
OF
THE GOLDEN GATE

PROLOGUE

IN San Francisco the 'rainy season' had been making itself a reality to the wondering Eastern immigrant. There were short days of drifting clouds and flying sunshine, and long succeeding nights of incessant downpour, when the rain rattled on the thin shingles or drummed on the resounding zinc of pioneer roofs. The shifting sand-dunes on the outskirts were beaten motionless and sodden by the onslaught of consecutive storms; the south-east trades brought the saline breath of the outlying Pacific even to the busy haunts of Commercial and Kearney Streets; the low-lying Mission-road was a quagmire; along the City Front, despite of piles and pier and wharf, the Pacific tides still asserted themselves in mud and ooze as far as Sansome Street; the wooden side-walks of Clay and Montgomery Streets were mere floating bridges or buoyant pontoons superposed on elastic bogs; Battery Street was the Silurian beach of that early period on which tin cans, packing-boxes, freight, household furniture, and even the runaway crews of deserted ships had been cast away. There were dangerous and unknown depths in Montgomery Street and on the Plaza, and the wheels of a passing carriage hopelessly mired had to be lifted by the volunteer hands of a half-dozen high-booted wayfarers, whose wearers were sufficiently content to believe that a woman, a child, or an invalid was behind its closed windows, without troubling themselves or the occupant by looking through the glass.

It was a carriage that, thus released, eventually drew up before the superior public edifice known as the City Hall. From it a woman, closely veiled, alighted, and quickly entered the building. A few passers-by turned to look at her, partly from the rarity of the female figure at that period, and partly from the greater rarity of its being well-formed and even lady-like.

As she kept her way along the corridor and ascended an iron staircase, she was passed by others more pre-occupied in business at the various public offices. One of these visitors, however, stopped as if struck by some fancied resemblance in her appearance, turned, and followed her. But when she halted before a door marked 'Mayor's Office,' he paused also, and, with a look of half-humorous bewilderment and a slight glance around him as if seeking for someone to whom to impart his arch fancy, he turned away. The woman then entered a large ante-room with a certain quick feminine gesture of relief, and, finding it empty of other callers, summoned the porter, and asked him some question in a voice so suppressed by the official severity of the apartment as to be hardly audible. The attendant replied by entering another room marked 'Mayor's Secretary,' and reappeared with a stripling of

She halted before a door marked 'Mayor's Office'

seventeen or eighteen, whose singularly bright eyes were all that was youthful in his composed features. After a slight scrutiny of the woman

'Certainly. That's motive enough—ain't it?'

'Yes.' The Mayor took his feet off his companion's chair and sat upright. Colonel Pendleton did the same, also removing his cigar from his lips. 'I suppose you'll think this thing over?' he added.

'No—I want it done *now*—right here—in this office.'

'But you know it will be irrevocable.'

'That's what I want it to be—something might happen afterwards.'

'But you are leaving nothing for yourself, and if you are going to devote everything to this daughter, and lead a different life, you'll'——

'Who said I was?'

The two men paused, and looked at her.

'Look here, boys, you don't understand. From the day that paper is signed, I've nothing to do with the child. She passes out of my hands into yours, to be schooled, educated, and made a rich girl out of—and never to know who or what or where *I* am. She doesn't know now. I haven't given her and myself away in that style—you bet! She thinks I'm only a friend. She hasn't seen me more than once or twice, and not to know me again. Why, I was down there the other day, and passed her walking out with the Sisters and the other scholars, and she didn't know me—though one of the Sisters did. But they're mum—*they* are, and don't let on. Why, now I think of it, *you* were down there, Jack, presiding in big style as Mr. Mayor at the exercises. You must have noticed her. Little thing, about nine—lot of hair, the same colour as mine, and brown eyes. White and yellow sash. Had a necklace on of real pearls I gave her. *I bought them*, you understand, myself at Tucker's—gave two hundred and fifty dollars for them—and a big bouquet of white rosebuds and lilacs I sent her.'

'I remember her now on the platform,' said the Mayor, gravely. 'So that is your child?'

'You bet—no slouch either. But that's neither here nor there. What I want now is you and Harry to look after her and her property the same as if I didn't live. More than that, as if I had *never lived*. I've come to you two boys, because I reckon you're square men and won't give me away. But I want to fix it even firmer than that. I want you to take hold of this trust not as Jack Hammersley, but as the *Mayor of San Francisco*! And when you make way for a new Mayor, *he* takes up the trust by virtue of his office, you see, so there's a trustee all along. I reckon there'll always be a San Francisco and always a Mayor —at least till the child's of age ; and it gives her from the start a father, and a pretty big one too. Of course the new man isn't to know the why and wherefore of this. It's enough for him to take on that duty with his others, without asking questions. And he's only got to invest that money and pay it out as it's wanted, and consult Harry at times.'

The two men looked at each other with approving intelligence. 'But have you thought of a successor for *me*, in case somebody shoots me on sight any time in the next ten years?' asked Pendleton, with a gravity equal to her own.

'I reckon, as you're President of the El Dorado Bank, you'll make that a part of every president's duty too. You'll get the directors to agree to it, just as Jack here will get the

Common Council to make it the Mayor's business.'

The two men had risen to their feet, and, after exchanging glances, gazed at her silently. Presently the Mayor said——

'It can be done, Kate, and we'll do it for you—eh, Harry?'

'Count me in,' said Pendleton, nodding.

'But you'll want a third man.'

'What's that for?'

'The casting vote in case of any difficulty.'

The woman's face fell. 'I reckoned to keep it a secret with only you two,' she said half-bitterly.

'No matter. We'll find someone to act, or you'll think of somebody and let us know.'

'But I wanted to finish this thing right here,' she said impatiently. She was silent for a moment, with her arched black brows knitted. Then she said abruptly, 'Who's that smart little chap that let me in? He looks as if he might be trusted.'

'That's Paul Hathaway, my secretary. He's sensible, but too young. Stop! I don't know about that. There's no legal age necessary, and he's got an awfully old head on him,' said the Mayor, thoughtfully.

'And *I* say his youth's in his favour,' said Colonel Pendleton, promptly. 'He's been brought up in San Francisco, and he's got no d——d old-fashioned Eastern notions to get rid of, and will drop into this as a matter of business, without prying about or wondering. *I'll* serve with him.'

'Call him in!' said the woman.

He came. Very luminous of eye, and composed of lip and brow; yet with the same suggestion of 'making believe' very much, as if to offset the possible munching of forbidden cakes and apples in his own room, or the hidden presence of some still in his pocket.

The Mayor explained the case briefly, but with business-like precision. 'Your duty, Mr. Hathaway,' he concluded, 'at present will be merely nominal and, above all, confidential. Colonel Pendleton and myself will set the thing going.' As the youth—who had apparently taken in and 'illuminated' the whole subject with a single bright-eyed glance—bowed and was about to retire, as if to relieve himself of his real feelings behind the door, the woman stopped him with a gesture.

'Let's have this thing over now,' she said to the Mayor. 'You draw up something that we can all sign at once.' She fixed her eyes on Paul, partly to satisfy her curiosity and justify her predilection for him, and partly to detect him in any overt act of boyishness. But the youth simply returned her glance with a cheerful, easy prescience, as if her past lay clearly open before him. For some minutes there was only the rapid scratching of the Mayor's pen over the paper. Suddenly he stopped and looked up.

'What's her name?'

'She musn't have mine,' said the woman quickly. 'That's a part of my idea. I give that up with the rest. She must take a new name that gives no hint of me. Think of one, can't you, you two men? Something that would kind of show that she was the daughter of the city, you know.'

'You couldn't call her "Santa Francisca," eh?' said Colonel Pendleton, doubtingly.

'Not much,' said the woman, with a seriousness that defied any ulterior insinuation.

For some minutes there was only the rapid scratching of the Mayor's pen

'Nor Chrysopolinia?' said the Mayor, musingly.

'But that's only a *first* name. She must have a family name,' said the woman, impatiently.

'Can *you* think of something, Paul?' said the Mayor, appealing to Hathaway. 'You're a great reader, and later from your classics than I am.' The Mayor, albeit practical and Western, liked to be ostentatiously forgetful of his old Alma Mater, Harvard, on occasions.

'How would *Yerba Buena* do, Sir?' responded the youth gravely. 'It's the old Spanish title of the first settlement here. It comes from the name that Father Junipero Serra gave to the pretty little vine that grows wild over the sandhills, and means "Good herb." He called it "A balm for the wounded and sore."'

'For the wounded and sore?' repeated the woman slowly.

'That's what they say,' responded Hathaway.

'You ain't playing us, eh?' she said, with a half-laugh that, however, scarcely curved the open mouth with which she had been regarding the young secretary.

'No,' said the Mayor, hurriedly. 'It's true. I've often heard it. And a capital name it would be for her too. *Yerba* the first name, *Buena* the second. She could be called Miss Buena when she grows up.'

'Yerba Buena it is,' she said suddenly. Then, indicating the youth with a slight toss of her handsome head. 'His head's level—you can see that.'

There was a silence again, and the scratching of the Mayor's pen continued. Colonel Pendleton buttoned up his coat, pulled his long moustache into shape, slightly arranged his collar, and walked to the window without looking at the woman. Presently the Mayor arose from his seat, and, with a certain formal courtesy that had been wanting in his previous manner, handed her his pen and arranged his chair for her at the desk. She took the pen, and rapidly appended her signature to the paper. The others followed, and, obedient to a sign from him, the porter was summoned from the outer office to witness the signatures. When this was over, the Mayor turned to his secretary, 'That's all just now, Paul.'

Accepting this implied dismissal with undisturbed gravity, the newly made youthful guardian bowed and retired. When the greenbaize door had closed upon him, the Mayor turned abruptly to the woman with the paper in his hand.

'Look here, Kate; there is still time for you to reconsider your action, and tear up this solitary record of it. If you choose to do so, say so, and I promise you that this interview, and all you have told us, shall never pass beyond these walls. No one will be the wiser for it, and we will give you full credit for having attempted something that was too much for you to perform.'

She had half-risen from her chair when he began, but fell back again in her former position and looked impatiently from him to his companion, who was also regarding her earnestly.

'What are you talking about?' she said sharply.

'*You*, Kate,' said the Mayor. 'You have given everything you possess to this child. What provision have you made for yourself?'

'Do I look played out?' she said, facing them.

She certainly did not look like anything but

a strong, handsome, resolute woman; but the men did not reply.

'That is not all, Kate,' continued the Mayor, folding his arms and looking down upon her. 'Have you thought what this means? It is the complete renunciation not only of any claim but any interest in your child. That is what you have just signed, and what it will be our duty now to keep you to. From this moment we stand between you and her, as we stand between her and the world. Are you ready to see her grow up away from you, losing even the little recollection she has had of your kindness—passing you in the street without knowing you, perhaps even having you pointed out to her as a person she should avoid? Are you prepared to shut your eyes and ears henceforth to all that you may hear of her new life, when she is happy, rich, respectable, a courted heiress—perhaps the wife of some great man? Are you ready to accept that she will never know—that no one will ever know—that *you* had any share in making her so, and that if you should ever breathe it abroad we shall hold it our duty to deny it, and brand the man who takes it up for you as a liar and the slanderer of an honest girl?'

'That's what I came here for,' she said curtly; then, regarding them curiously, and running her ringed hand up and down the railed back of her chair, she added, with a half-laugh, 'What are you playin' me for, boys?'

'But,' said Colonel Pendleton, without heeding her, 'are you ready to know that in sickness or affliction you will be powerless to help her; that a stranger will take your place at her bedside, that as she has lived without knowing you she will die without that knowledge, or that if through any weakness of yours it came to her then, it would embitter her last thoughts of earth and, dying, she would curse you?'

The smile upon her half-open mouth still fluttered around it, and her curved fingers still ran up and down the rails of the chair-back as if they were the chords of some mute instrument, to which she was trying to give voice. Her rings once or twice grated upon them as if she had at times gripped them closely. But she rose quickly when he paused, said 'Yes' sharply, and put the chair back against the wall.

'Then I will send you copies of this tomorrow, and take an assignment of the property.'

'I've got the check here for it now,' she

'Do you know who that woman is?'

said, drawing it from her pocket and laying it upon the desk. 'There, I reckon that's finished. Good-bye!'

The Mayor took up his hat, Colonel Pendleton did the same; both men preceded her to the door, and held it open with grave politeness for her to pass.

'Where are you boys going?' she asked, glancing from the one to the other.

'To see you to your carriage, Mrs. Howard,' said the Mayor, in a voice that had become somewhat deeper.

'Through the whole building? Past all the people in the hall and on the stairs? Why, I passed Dan Stewart as I came in.'

'If you will allow us?' he said, turning half-appealingly to Colonel Pendleton, who without speaking, made a low bow of assent.

A slight flush rose to her face—the first and only change in the even healthy colour she had shown during the interview.

'I reckon I won't trouble you, boys, if it's all the same to you,' she said, with her half-strident laugh. '*You* mightn't mind being seen —but *I* would—Good-bye.'

She held out a hand to each of the men, who remained for an instant silently holding them. Then she passed out of the door, slipping on her close black veil as she did so with a half-funereal suggestion, and they saw her tall handsome figure fade into the shadows of the long corridor.

'Paul,' said the Mayor, re-entering the office and turning to his secretary, 'do you know who that woman is?'

'Yes, Sir.'

'She's one in a million! And now forget that you have ever seen her.'

CHAPTER I

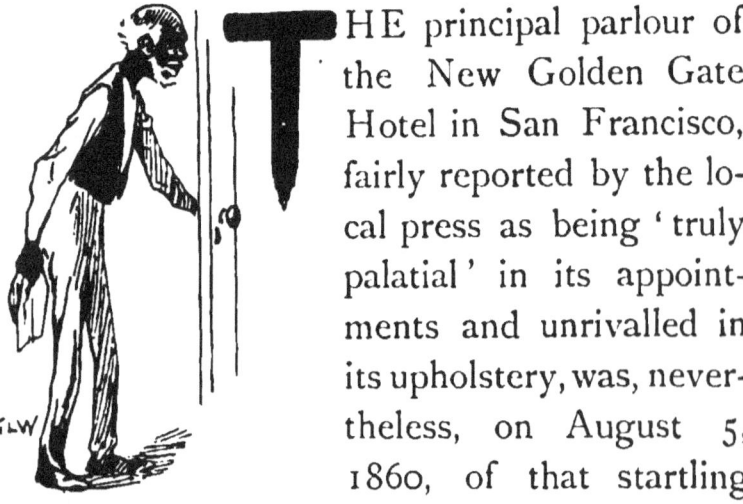

THE principal parlour of the New Golden Gate Hotel in San Francisco, fairly reported by the local press as being 'truly palatial' in its appointments and unrivalled in its upholstery, was, nevertheless, on August 5, 1860, of that startling newness that checked any familiarity, and evidently had produced some embarrassment in the limbs of four visitors who had just been ushered into its glories. After hesitating before one or two gorgeous fawn-coloured brocaded easy-chairs of appalling and spotless virginity, one of them seated himself despairingly on a tête-à-tête sofa in marked and painful isolation, while another sat uncomfortably upright on a sofa. The two others remained standing, vaguely gazing at the ceiling, and exchanging ostentatiously admiring but hollow remarks about the furniture in unnecessary whispers. Yet they were apparently men of a certain habit of importance and small authority, with more or less critical attitude in their speech.

To them presently entered a young man of about five-and-twenty, with remarkably bright and singularly sympathetic eyes. Having swept the group in a smiling glance, he singled out the lonely occupier of the tête-à-tête, and moved pleasantly towards him. The man rose instantly with an eager gratified look.

'Well, Paul, I didn't allow you'ld remember me. It's a matter of four years since we met at Marysville. And now you're bein' a great man you've . .'

No one could have known from the young man's smiling face that he really had not recognised his visitor at first, and that his greeting was only an exhibition of one of those happy instincts for which he was remarkable. But, following the clue suggested by his visitor, he was able to say promptly and gaily—

'I don't know why I should forget Tony Shear or the Marysville boys,' turning with a

'I didn't allow you'ld remember me'

half-confiding smile to the other visitors, who, after the human fashion, were beginning to be resentfully impatient of this special attention.

'Well, no—for I've allus said that you took your first start from Marysville. But I've brought a few friends of our Party—that I reckoned to introduce to you. Cap'en Stidger, Chairman of our Central Committee, Mr. Henry J. Hoskins, of the firm of Hoskins and Bloomer, and Joe Slate, of the 'Union Press,' one of our most promising journalists. Gentlemen,' he continued, suddenly and without warning lifting his voice to an oratorical plane in startling contrast to his previous unaffected utterance, 'I needn't say that this is the Honourable Paul Hathaway—the youngest State Senator in the Legislature. You know his record!' Then recovering the ordinary accents of humanity, he added, 'We read of your departure last night from Sacramento, and I thought we'd come early, afore the crowd.'

'Proud to know you, Sir,' said Captain Stidger, suddenly lifting the conversation to the platform again. 'I have followed your career, Sir. I've read your speech, Mr. Hathaway, and, as I was telling our mutual friend, Mr. Shear, as we came along, I don't know any man that could state the real Party issues as squarely.

Your castigating exposition of so-called Jeffersonian principles, and your relentless indictment of the resolutions of '98, were—were '—coughed the Captain, dropping into conversation again —' were the biggest thing out. You have only to signify the day, Sir, that you will address us, and I can promise you the largest audience in San Francisco.'

'I'm instructed by the proprietor of the *Union Press*,' said Mr. Slate, feeling for his notebook and pencil, 'to offer you its columns for any explanations you may desire to make in the form of a personal letter or an editorial in reply to the *Advertiser's* strictures on your speech, or to take any information you may have for the benefit of our readers and the Party.'

'If you are ever down my way, Mr. Hathaway,' said Mr. Hoskins, placing a large business card in Hathaway's hand, 'and will drop in as a friend, I can show you about the largest business in the way of canned provisions and domestic groceries in the State, and give you a look around Battery-street generally. Or if you'll name your day, I've got a pair of 2·35 Blue Grass horses that'll spin you out to the Cliff House to dinner and back. I've had Governor Fiske, and Senator Doolan, and that big English capitalist who was here last year, and they—well, Sir—they were *pleased*! Or if you'd like to see the town—if this is your first visit—I'm on hand to show you.'

Nothing could exceed Mr. Hathaway's sympathetic acceptance of their courtesies, nor was there the least affectation in it. Thoroughly enjoying his fellow-men, even in their foibles, they found him irresistibly attractive. 'I lived here seven years ago,' he said, smilingly, to the speaker.

'When the water came up to Montgomery-street,' interposed Mr. Shear, in a hoarse but admiring aside.

'When Mr. Hammersley was Mayor,' continued Hathaway.

'Had an official position—private secretary—afore he was twenty,' explained Shear, in perfectly audible confidence.

'Since then the City has made great strides, leaping full-grown, Sir, in a single night,' said

Captain Stidger, hastily ascending the rostrum again with a mixed metaphor, to the apparent concern of a party of handsomely dressed young ladies who had recently entered the parlour. 'Stretching from South Park to Black Point, and running back to the Mission Dolores and the Presidio, we are building up a metropolis, Sir, worthy to be placed beside the Golden Gate that opens to the broad Pacific and the shores of far Cathay! When the Pacific Railroad is built we shall be the natural terminus of the Pathway of Nations!'

Mr. Hathaway's face betrayed no consciousness that he had heard something like this eight years before, and that much of it had come true, as he again sympathetically responded. Neither was his attention attracted by a singular similarity which the attitude of the group of ladies on the other side of the parlour bore to that of his own party. They were clustered around one of their own number—a striking-looking girl—who was apparently receiving their mingled flatteries and caresses with a youthful yet critical sympathy which, singularly enough, was not unlike his own. It was evident also that an odd sort of rivalry seemed to spring up between the two parties, and that, in proportion as Hathaway's admirers became more marked and ostentatious in their attentions, the supporters of the young girl were equally effusive and enthusiastic in their devotion. As usual in such cases, the real contest was between the partisans themselves; each successive demonstration on either side was provocative or retaliatory, and when they were apparently rendering homage to their idols they were really distracted by and listening to each other. At last, Hathaway's party being reinforced by fresh visitors, a tall brunette of the opposition remarked in a professedly confidential but perfectly audible tone—

'Well, my dear, as I don't suppose you want to take part in a political caucus, perhaps we'd better return to the Ladies' Boudoir, unless there's a committee sitting there too.'

'I know how valuable your time must be, as you are all business men,' said Hathaway, turning to his party, in an equally audible tone; 'but before you go, gentlemen, you must let me offer you a little refreshment in a private room,' and he moved naturally towards the door. The rival fair, who had already risen at their commander's suggestion, here paused awkwardly over an embarrassing victory. Should they go or stay? The object of their devotion, however, turned curiously towards Hathaway. For an instant their eyes met. The young girl turned carelessly to her companions and said: 'No; stay here—it's the public parlour,' and her followers, evidently accustomed to her authority, sat down again.

'A galaxy of young ladies from the Convent of Santa Clara, Mr. Hathaway,' explained Captain Stidger, naïvely oblivious of any discourtesy on their part, as he followed Hathaway's glance and took his arm as they moved away. 'Not the least of our treasures, Sir. Most of them daughters of pioneers—and all Californian bred and educated. Connoisseurs have awarded them the palm, and declare that for Grace, Intelligence, and Woman's Highest Charms the East cannot furnish their equal.' Having delivered this Parthian compliment in an oratorical passage through the doorway, the Captain descended, outside, into familiar speech.

'But I suppose you will find that out for yourself if you stay here long. San Francisco might furnish a fitting bride to California's youngest Senator.'

'I am afraid that my stay here must be brief, and limited to business,' said Hathaway, who had merely noticed that the principal girl was handsome and original-looking. 'In fact, I am here partly to see an old acquaintance—Colonel Pendleton.'

The three men looked at each other curiously. 'Oh! Harry Pendleton, said Mr. Hoskins, incredulously. 'You don't know *him*?'

'An old pioneer—of course,' interposed Shear, explanatorily and apologetically. 'Why, in Paul's time the Colonel was a big man here.'

'I understand the Colonel has been unfortunate,' said Hathaway gravely; 'but, in *my* time, he was President of the El Dorado Bank.'

'And the bank hasn't got through its settlement yet,' said Hoskins. 'I hope *you* ain't expecting to get anything out of it?'

'No,' said Hathaway, smiling; 'I was a boy at that time, and lived up to my salary. I know nothing of his bank difficulties, but it always struck me that Colonel Pendleton was himself an honourable man.'

'It ain't that,' said Captain Stidger, energetically, 'but the trouble with Harry Pendleton is that he hasn't grown with the State, and never adjusted himself to it. And he won't. He thinks the Millennium was between the fall of '49 and the spring of '50, and after that everything dropped. He belongs to the old days, when a man's simple *word* was good for any amount if you knew him; and they say that the old bank hadn't a scrap of paper for half that was owing to it. That was all very well, Sir, in '49 and '50, and—Luck; but it won't do for '59 and '60, and—Business! And the old man can't see it.'

'But he is ready to fight for it now, as in the old time,' said Mr. Slate, 'and that's another trouble with his chronology. He's done more to keep up duelling than any other man in the State, and don't know the whole spirit of progress and civilisation is against it.'

It was impossible to tell from Paul Hathaway's face whether his sympathy with Colonel

Tended to increase their good humour

Pendleton's foibles or his assent to the criticisms of his visitors was the truer. Both were no doubt equally sincere. But the party was presently engaged in the absorption of refreshment, which, being of a purely spirituous and exhilarating quality, tended to increase their good humour with the host till they parted. Even then a gratuitous advertisement of his virtues and their own intentions in calling upon him was oratorically voiced from available platforms and landings, in the halls and stairways, until it was pretty well known throughout the Golden Gate Hotel that the Hon. Mr. Paul Hathaway had arrived from Sacramento, and had received a 'spontaneous ovation.'

Meantime the object of it had dropped into an easy-chair by the window of his room, and was endeavouring to recall a less profitable memory. The process of human forgetfulness is not a difficult one between the ages of eighteen and twenty-six, and Paul Hathaway had not only fulfilled the Mayor's request by forgetting the particulars of a certain transfer that he had witnessed in the Mayor's office, but in the year succeeding that request, being about to try his fortunes in the mountains, he had formally constituted Colonel Pendleton to act as his proxy in the administration of

Mrs. Howard's singular Trust, in which, however, he had never participated except yearly to sign his name. He was, consequently, somewhat astonished to have received a letter a few days before from Colonel Pendleton, asking him to call and see him regarding it.

He vaguely remembered that it was eight years ago, and eight years had worked considerable change in the original trustees, greatest of all in his superior officer, the Mayor, who had died the year following, leaving his trusteeship to his successor in office, whom Paul Hathaway had never seen. The Bank of El Dorado, despite Mrs. Howard's sanguine belief, had long been in bankruptcy, and, although Colonel Pendleton still survived it, it was certain that no other president would succeed to his office as trustee, and that the function would lapse with him. Paul himself, a soldier of fortune, although habitually lucky, had only lately succeeded to a profession—if his political functions could be so described. Even with his luck, energy, and ambition, while everything was possible, nothing was secure. It seemed, therefore, as if the soulless official must eventually assume the duties of the two sympathising friends who had originated them, and had stood *in loco parentis* to the constructive orphan. The mother, Mrs. Howard, had disappeared a year after the Trust had been made—it was charitably presumed in order to prevent any complications that might arise from her presence in the country. With these facts before him, Paul Hathaway was more concerned in wondering what Pendleton could want with him than, I fear, any direct sympathy with the situation. On the contrary, it appeared to him more favourable for keeping the secret of Mrs. Howard's relationship, which would now die with Colonel Pendleton and himself; and there was no danger of any emotional betrayal of it in the cold official administration of a man who had received the Trust through the formal hands of successive predecessors. He had forgotten the time limited for the guardianship, but the girl must soon be of age and off their hands. If there had ever been any romantic or chivalrous impression left upon his memory by the scene in the Mayor's office, I fear he had put it away with various other foolish illusions of his youth, to which he now believed he was superior.

Nevertheless, he would see the Colonel, and at once, and settle the question. He looked at the address, 'St. Charles' Hotel.' He remembered an old hostelry of that name, near the Plaza. Could it be possible that it had survived the alterations and improvements of the city? It was an easy walk through remembered streets, yet with changed shops and houses and faces. When he reached the Plaza, scarce recognisable in its later frontages of brick and stone, he found the old wooden building still intact, with its villa-like galleries and verandahs incongruously and ostentatiously overlooked by two new and aspiring erections on either side. For an instant he tried to recall the glamour of old days. He remembered when his boyish eyes regarded it as the crowning work of opulence and distinction; he remembered a ball given there on some public occasion, which was to him the acme of social brilliancy and display. How tawdry and trivial it looked beside those later and more solid structures! How inconsistent were those long latticed verandahs and balconies, pathetic record of that first illusion of the pioneers that their climate was a tropical one! A restaurant and billiard-saloon had aggrandised all of the lower storey; but there was still the fanlight, over which the remembered title of 'St. Charles,' in gilded letters, was now reinforced by the too demonstrative legend, 'Apartments and Board, by the Day or Week.' Was it possible that this narrow, creaking staircase had once seemed to him the broad steps of Fame and Fortune? On the first landing, a preoccupied Irish servant-girl, with a mop, directed him to a door at the end of the passage, at which he knocked. The door was opened by a grizzled negro servant, who was still holding a piece of oily chamois-leather in his hand; and the contents of a duelling-case, scattered upon a table in the centre of the room, showed what had been his occupation. Admitting Hathaway with great courtesy, he said—

'Marse Harry bin havin' his ole trubble, Sah, and bin engaged just dis momen' on his toylet; ef yo'll accommodate yo'self on de sofa, I inform him yo is heah.'

As the negro passed into the next room, Paul cast a hasty glance around the apartment. The furniture, originally rich and elegant, was now worn threadbare and lustreless. A bookcase, containing, among other volumes, a few law books—there being a vague tradition, as Paul remembered, that Colonel Pendleton had once been connected with the law—a few French chairs of tarnished gilt; a rifle in the corner, a presentation sword in a mahogany case, a few classical prints on the walls, and one or two iron deed-boxes marked 'El Dorado Bank,' were the principal objects. A mild flavour of dry decay and methylated spirits pervaded the apartment. Yet it was scrupulously clean and well kept, and a few clothes neatly brushed and folded on a chair bore witness to the servant's care. As Paul, however, glanced behind the sofa, he was concerned to see a coat, which had evidently been thrust hurriedly in a corner, with the sleeve lining inside out, and a needle and thread still sticking in the seam. It struck him instantly that this had been the negro's occupation, and that the pistol-cleaning was a polite fiction.

'Yo'll have to skuse Marse Harry seein' yo in bed, but his laig's pow'ful bad to-day, and he can't stand,' said the servant, re-entering the room. 'Skuse me, Sah,' he added in a dignified confidential whisper, half-closing the door with his hand, 'but if yo wouldn't mind avoidin' 'xcitin' or controversical topics in yo' conversation it would be de better fo' him.'

Paul smilingly assented, and the black retainer, with even more than the usual solemn ceremonious exaggeration of his race, ushered him into the bedroom. It was furnished in the same faded glory as the sitting-room, with the exception of a low iron camp-bedstead, in which the tall soldierly figure of Colonel Pendleton, clad in threadbare silk dressing-gown, was stretched. He had changed in eight years; his hair had become grey, and was thinned over the sunken temples, but his iron-grey moustache was still particularly long and well pointed. His face bore marks of illness and care; there were deep lines down the angle of the nostril that spoke of alternate savage outbreak and repression, and gave his smile a sardonic rigidity. His dark eyes, that shone with the exaltation of fever, fixed Paul's on entering, and with the tyranny of an invalid never left them.

'Well, Hathaway?'

With the sound of that voice Paul felt the years slip away, and he was again a boy, looking up admiringly to the strong man, who now lay helpless before him. He had entered the room with a faint sense of sympathising superiority and a consciousness of having had experience in controlling men. But all this fled before Colonel Pendleton's authoritative voice; even its broken tones carried the old dominant spirit of the man, and Paul found himself admiring a quality in his old acquaintance that he missed in his newer friends.

'I haven't seen you for eight years, Hathaway. Come here and let me look at you.'

Paul approached the bedside with boyish obedience. Pendleton took his hand and gazed at him critically.

'I should have recognised you, Sir, for all your moustache and your inches. The last time I saw you was in Jack Hammersley's office. Well, Jack's dead, and here *I* am, little better, I reckon. You remember Hammersley's house?'

'Yes,' said Paul, albeit wondering at the question.

'Something like this, Swiss villa style. I remember when Jack put it up. Well, the last time I was out, I passed there. And what do you think they've done to it?'

Paul could not imagine.

'Well, Sir,' said the Colonel gravely, 'they've changed it into a Church Missionary shop and Young Men's Christian Reading-room! But, that's "progress" and "improvement"!' He paused, and, slowly withdrawing his hand from Paul's, added with grim apology: 'You're young, and belong to the new school, perhaps. Well, Sir, I've read your speech; I don't belong to your Party—mine died ten years ago—but I congratulate you. George! Confound it! where's that boy gone?'

The negro indicated by this youthful title, although he must have been ten years older than his master, after a hurried shuffling in the sitting-room, eventually appeared at the door.

'George, champagne and materials for

cocktails for the gentleman. The *best*, you understand. No new-fangled notions from that new barkeeper.'

Paul, who thought he observed a troubled blinking in George's eyelid, and referred it to a fear of possible excitement for his patient, here begged his host not to trouble himself—that he seldom took anything in the morning.

'Possibly not, Sir; possibly not,' returned the Colonel, hastily. 'I know the new ideas are prohibitive and some other blank thing, but you're safe here from your constituents, and by gad, Sir, I shan't force you to take it! It's *my* custom, Hathaway—an old one—played out, perhaps, like all the others, but a custom nevertheless, and I'm only surprised that George, who knows it, should have forgotten it.'

'Fack is, Marse Harry,' said George, with feverish apology, 'it bin gone 'scaped my mind dis mo'nin' in de prerogation ob business, but I'm goin' now shuah!' and he disappeared.

'A good boy, Sir, but beginning to be contaminated. Brought him here from Nashville over ten years ago. Eight years ago they proved to him that he was no longer a slave, and made him d——d unhappy until I promised him it should make no difference to him and he could stay. I had to send for his wife and child—of course, a dead loss of eighteen hundred dollars when they set foot in the State—but I'm blanked if he isn't just as miserable with them here, for he has to take two hours in the morning and three in the afternoon every day to be with 'em. I tried to get him to take his family to the mines and make his fortune, like those fellows they call bankers and operators and stockbrokers nowadays; or to go to Oregon, where they'll make him some kind of a mayor or sheriff—but he won't. He collects my rents on some little property I have left, and pays my bills, Sir, and, if this blank civilisation would only leave him alone, he'd be a good enough boy.'

Paul couldn't help thinking that the rents George collected were somewhat inconsistent with those he was evidently mending when he arrived, but at that moment the jingle of glasses was heard in the sitting-room, and the old negro reappeared at the door. Drawing himself up with ceremonious courtesy, he addressed Paul.

'Wo'd yo mind, Sah, taking a glance at de wine for yo' choice?' Paul rose, and followed

'De Kernel won't have any but de best champagne'

him into the sitting-room, when George carefully closed the door. To his surprise Hathaway beheld a tray with two glasses of whisky and bitters, but no wine. 'Skuse me, Sah,' said the old man with dignified apology, 'but de Kernel won't have any but de best champagne for hono'ble gemmen like yo'self, and I'se despaired to say it kan't be got in de house or de subburbs. De best champagne dat we gives visitors is the Widder Glencoe. Wo'd yo mind, Sah, for de sake o' not 'xcitin' de Kernel wid triflin' culinary matter, to say dat yo don' take but de one brand?'

'Certainly,' said Paul, smiling. 'I really don't care for anything so early,' then, returning to the bedroom, he said carelessly, 'You'll excuse me taking the liberty, Colonel, of sending away the champagne and contenting myself with whisky. Even the best brand—the Widow Cliquot'—with a glance at the gratified George—'I find rather trying so early in the morning.'

'As you please, Hathaway,' said the Colonel, somewhat stiffly. 'I dare say there's a new fashion in drinks now, and a gentleman's stomach is a thing of the past. Then, I suppose, we can spare the boy, as this is his time for going home. Put that tin box with the

Trust papers on the bed, George, and Mr. Hathaway will excuse your waiting.' As the old servant made an exaggerated obeisance to each, Paul remarked, as the door closed upon him, 'George certainly keeps his style, Colonel, in the face of the progress you deplore.'

'He was always a "dandy nigger,"' returned Pendleton, his face slightly relaxing as he glanced after his grizzled henchman, 'but his exaggeration of courtesy is a blank sight more natural and manly than the exaggeration of discourtesy which your superior civilised "helps" think is self-respect. The excuse of servitude of any kind is its spontaneity and affection. When you know a man hates you and serves you from interest, you know he's a cur and you're a tyrant. It's your blank progress that's made menial service degrading by teaching men to avoid it. Why, Sir, when I first arrived here, Jack Hammersley and myself took turns as cook to the party. I didn't consider myself any the worse master for it. But enough of this.' He paused, and, raising himself on his elbow, gazed for some seconds half-cautiously, half-doubtfully, upon his companion.

'I've got something to tell you, Hathaway,' he said slowly. 'You've had an easy time with this Trust; your share of the work hasn't worried you, kept you awake nights, or interfered with your career. I understand perfectly,' he continued, in reply to Hathaway's deprecating gesture. 'I accepted to act as your proxy, and I *have*. I'm not complaining. But it is time that you should know what I've done, and what you may still have to do. Here is the record. On the day after that interview in the Mayor's office, the El Dorado Bank, of which I was, and still am, president, received seventy-five thousand dollars in trust from Mrs. Howard. Two years afterwards, on that same day, the bank had, by lucky speculations, increased that sum to the credit of the trust one hundred and fifty thousand dollars, or double the original capital. In the following year the bank suspended payment.'

CHAPTER II

IN an instant the whole situation and his relations to it flashed upon Paul with a terrible, but almost grotesque, completeness. Here he was, at the outset of his career, responsible for the wasted fortune of the daughter of a social outcast, and saddled with her support! He now knew why Colonel Pendleton had wished to see him; for one shameful moment he believed he also knew why he had been content to take his proxy! The questionable character of the whole transaction, his own carelessness, which sprang from that very confidence and trust that Pendleton had lately extolled—what *would*, what *could* not be made of it! He already heard himself abused by his opponents—perhaps, more terrible still, faintly excused by his friends. All this was visible in his pale face and flashing eyes as he turned them on the helpless invalid.

Colonel Pendleton received his look with the same critical, half-curious scrutiny that had accompanied his speech. At last his face changed slightly, a faint look of disappointment crossed his eyes and a sardonic smile deepened the lines of his mouth.

'There, Sir,' he said hurriedly, as if dismissing an unpleasant revelation; 'don't alarm yourself! Take a drink of that whisky. You look pale. Well; turn your eyes on those walls. You don't see any of that money laid out here—do you? Look at me. I don't look like a man enriched with other people's money —do I? Well, let that content you. Every dollar of that Trust fund, Hathaway, with all the interests and profits that have accrued to it, is *safe*! Every cent of it is locked up in Government Bonds with Rothschild's agent. There are the receipts, dated a week before the bank suspended. But enough of *that—that* isn't what I asked you to come and see me for.'

The blood had rushed back to Paul's cheeks uncomfortably. He saw now, as impulsively as he had previously suspected his co-trustee, that the man had probably ruined himself to save the Trust. He stammered that he had not questioned the management of the fund nor asked to withdraw his proxy.

'No matter, Sir,' said the Colonel, impatiently; 'you had the right, and, I suppose,' he added with half-concealed scorn, 'it was your duty. But let that pass. The money is safe enough; but, Mr. Hathaway—and this is the point I want to discuss with you—it begins to look as if the *secret* was safe no longer!' He had raised himself with some pain and difficulty to draw nearer to Paul, and had again fixed his eyes eagerly upon him. But Paul's responsive glance was so vague that he added quickly: 'You understand, Sir; I believe that there are hounds—I say hounds!—who would be able to blurt out at any moment that that girl at Santa Clara is Kate Howard's daughter.'

At any other moment Paul might have

questioned the gravity of any such contingency, but the terrible earnestness of the speaker, his dominant tone, and a certain respect which had lately sprung up in his breast for him, checked him, and he only asked, with as much concern as he could master for the moment—

'What makes you think so?'

'That's what I want to tell you, Hathaway, and how I, and I alone, are responsible for it. When the bank was in difficulty and I made up my mind to guard the Trust with my own personal and private capital, I knew that there might be some comment on my action. It was a delicate matter to show any preference or exclusion at such a moment, and I took two or three of my brother directors whom I thought I could trust into my confidence, I told them the whole story, and how the Trust was sacred. I made a mistake, Sir,' continued Pendleton, sardonically, 'a grave mistake. I did not take into account that even in three years civilisation and religion had gained ground here. There was a hound there—a blank Judas in the Trust. Well; he didn't see it. I think he talked Scripture and morality. He said something about the wages of sin being infamous and only worthy of confiscation. He talked about the sins of the father being visited upon the children, and justly. I stopped him. Well! Do you know what's the matter with my ankle? Look!' He stopped and, with some difficulty and invincible gravity throwing aside his dressing-gown, turned down his stocking, and exposed to Paul's gaze the healed cicatrix of an old bullet-wound. 'Troubled me damnably near a year. Where I hit *him*—hasn't troubled him at all since!

'I think,' continued the Colonel, falling back upon the pillow with an air of relief, 'that he told others—of his own kidney, Sir—though it was a secret among gentlemen. But they have preferred to be silent now—than *afterwards*. They know that I'm ready. But I can't keep this up long; some time, you know, they're bound to improve in practice and hit higher up! As far as I'm concerned,' he added, with a grim glance around the faded walls and threadbare furniture, 'it don't mind; but *mine* isn't the mouth to be stopped.' He paused, and then abruptly, yet with a sudden and pathetic dropping of his dominant note, said: 'Hathaway, you're young, and Hammersley liked you—what's to be done? I thought of passing over my tools to you. You can shoot, and I hear you *have*. But the h—l of it is that if you dropped a man or two people would ask *why*, and want to know what it was about; while, when I do, nobody here thinks it anything but *my way*! I don't mean that it would hurt you with the crowd to wipe out one or two of these hounds during the canvass, but the trouble is that they belong to *your Party*, and,' he added grimly, 'that wouldn't help your career.'

'But,' said Paul, ignoring the sarcasm, 'are you not magnifying the effect of a disclosure? The girl is an heiress, excellently brought up. Who will bother about the antecedents of the mother, who has disappeared, whom she never knew, and who is legally dead to her?'

'In my day, Sir, no one who knew the circumstances,' returned the Colonel quickly. 'But we are living in a blessed era of Christian retribution and civilised propriety, and I believe there are a lot of men and women about who have no other way of showing their own virtue than by showing up another's vice. We're in a reaction of reform. It's the old drunkards who are always more clamorous for total abstinence than the moderately temperate. I tell you, Hathaway, there couldn't be an unluckier moment for our secret coming out.'

'But she will be of age soon.'

'In two months,'

'And sure to marry.'

'Marry!' repeated Pendleton, with grim irony. 'Would *you* marry her?'

'That's another question,' said the young man promptly, 'and one of individual taste; but it does not affect my general belief that she could easily find a husband as good and better.'

'Suppose she found one *before* the secret came out. Ought he to be told?'

'Certainly.'

'And that would imply telling *her*?'

'Yes,' said Paul, but not so promptly.

'And you consider *that* fulfilling the promise of the Trust—the pledges exchanged with that woman?' continued Pendleton, with glittering eyes and a return to his old dominant tone.

'My dear Colonel,' said Paul, somewhat less positively, but still smiling, 'you have made a romantic, almost impossible compact with Mrs. Howard, that you yourself are now obliged to admit, circumstances may prevent your carrying out substantially. You forget, also, that you have just told me that you have already broken your pledge—under circumstances, it is true, that do you honour—and that now your desperate attempts to retrieve it have failed. Now I really see nothing wrong in your telling to a presumptive well-wisher of the girl what you have told to her enemy.'

There was a dead silence. The prostrate man uttered a slight groan, as if in pain, and drew up his leg to change his position. After a pause, he said, in a restrained voice, 'I differ from you, Mr. Hathaway; but enough of this for the present. I have something else to say. It will be necessary for one of us to go at once to Santa Clara and see Miss Yerba Buena.'

'Good heavens!' said Paul, quickly. 'Do you call her *that?*'

'Certainly, Sir. *You* gave her the name. Have you forgotten?'

'I only suggested it,' returned Paul, hopelessly; 'but no matter—go on.'

'*I* cannot go there, as you see,' continued Pendleton, with a weary gesture towards his crippled ankle; 'and I should particularly like you to see her before we make the joint disposition of her affairs with the Mayor, two months hence. I have some papers you can show her, and I have already written a letter introducing you to the Lady Superior at the convent, and to her. You have never seen her?'

'No,' said Paul. 'But, of course, you have?'

'Not for three years.'

Paul's eyes evidently expressed some wonder, for a moment after the Colonel added, 'I believe, Hathaway, I am looked upon as a queer survival of a rather lawless and improper past. At least, I have thought it better not socially to compromise her by my presence. The Mayor goes there—at the examinations and exercises, I believe, Sir; they make a sort of reception for him—with a—a—banquet—lemonade and speeches.'

'I had intended to leave for Sacramento to-morrow night,' said Paul, glancing curiously at the helpless man; 'but I will go there if you wish.'

'Thank you. It will be better.'

There were a few words of further explanation of the papers, and Pendleton placed the packet in his visitor's hand. Paul rose. Somehow, it appeared to him that the room looked more faded and forgotten than when he entered it, and the figure of the man before him more lonely, helpless, and abandoned. With one of his sympathetic impulses he said—

'I don't like to leave you here alone. Are you sure you can help yourself without George? Can I do anything before I go?'

'I am quite accustomed to it,' said Pendleton, quietly. 'It happens once or twice a year, and when I go out—well—I miss more than I do here.'

He took Paul's proffered hand mechanically, with a slight return of the critical, doubting look he had cast upon him when he entered. His voice, too, had quite recovered its old dominance, as he said, with half-patronising conventionality, 'You'll have to find your way out

Pendleton placed the packet in his visitor's hand

alone. Let me know how you have sped at Santa Clara, will you? Good-bye.'

The staircase and passage seemed to have grown shabbier and meaner as Paul, slowly and hesitatingly, descended to the street. At the foot of the stairs he paused irresolutely, and loitered with a vague idea of turning back on some pretence, only that he might relieve himself of the sense of desertion. He had already determined upon making that inquiry into the Colonel's personal and pecuniary affairs which he had not dared to offer personally, and had a half-formed plan of testing his own power and popularity in a certain line of relief that at once satisfied his sympathies and ambitions. Nevertheless, after reaching the street, he lingered a moment, when an odd idea of temporising with his inclinations struck him. At the farther end of the hotel—one of the parasites living on its decayed fortunes—was a small barber's shop. By having his hair trimmed and his clothes brushed, he could linger a little longer beneath the same roof with the helpless solitary, and perhaps come to some conclusion. He entered the clean but scantily furnished shop, and threw himself into one of the nearest chairs, hardly noting that there were no other customers, and that a single assistant, stropping a razor behind a glass door, was the only occupant. But there was a familiar note of exaggerated politeness about the voice of this man as he opened the door and came towards the back of the chair with the formula—

'Mo'nin', Sah! Shall we hab de pleshure of shavin' or hah-cuttin' dis mo'nin'?' Paul raised his eyes quickly to the mirror before him. It reflected the black face and grizzled hair of George.

More relieved at finding the old servant still near his master than caring to comprehend the reason, Hathaway said pleasantly, 'Well, George, is this the way you look after your family?'

The old man started; for an instant his full red lips seemed to become dry and ashen, the whites of his eyes were suffused and staring, as he met Paul's smiling face in the glass. But almost as quickly he recovered himself, and, with a polite but deprecating bow, said—'For God sake, Sah! I admit de sarkumstances is agin me, but de simple fack is dat I'm temper'ly occupyin' de place of an ole frien', Sah, who is called round de cornah.'

'And I'm devilish glad of any fact, George,

that gives me a chance of having my hair cut by Colonel Pendleton's right-hand man. So fire away!'

He met Paul's smiling face in the glass

The gratified smile which now suddenly overspread the whole of the old man's face, and seemed to quickly stiffen the rugged and wrinkled fingers that had at first trembled in drawing a pair of shears from a ragged pocket, appeared to satisfy Paul's curiosity for the present. But after a few moments' silent snipping, during which he could detect in the mirror some traces of agitation still twitching the negro's face, he said with an air of conviction—

'Look here, George—why don't you regularly use your leisure moments in this trade? You'd make your fortune by your taste and skill at it.'

For the next half-minute the old man's frame shook with silent childlike laughter behind Paul's chair. 'Well, Marse Hathaway, yo's an ole frien' o' my massa, and a gemman yo'self, Sah, and a Senetah, and I do'an mind tellen' yo— dat's jess what I bin gone done! It makes a little ready money for de ole woman and de chillern. But de Kernel don' no'. Ah, Sah de Kernel kill me or hisself if he so much as spicioned me. De Kernel is high-toned, Sah! —being a gemman yo'self, yo' understand. He wouldn't heah of his niggah worken for two

F

Massas—for all he's agree'ble to lemme go and help mysef. But, Lord bless yo, Sah, dat ain't in de category! De Kernel couldn't get along widout me.'

'You collect his rents, don't you?' said Paul, quietly.

'Yes, Sah.'

'Much?'

'Well no, Sah; not so much as fom'ly, Sah! Yo see, de Kernel's prop'ty lies in de ole parts of de town, where de po' white folks lib, and dey ain't reg'lar. De Kernel dat sof' in his heart, he doant press 'em; some of 'em is ole fo'ty-niners like hisself, Sah; and some is Spanish, Sah, and dey is sof' too, and ain't no more gumption dan chillern, and tink it's ole time come agin, and dey's in de ole places like afo' de Mexican Wah! and dey don' bin' payin nffion'. But we gets along, Sah—we get's along, not in de *prima facie* style, Sah! mebbe not in de modden way dat de Kernel don't like; but we keeps ourse'f, Sah, and has wine fo' our friends. When yo' come again, Sah, yo'll find de Widder Glencoe on de sideboard.'

'Has the Colonel many friends here?'

'Mos' de ole ones bin done gone, Sah, and de Kernel don' cotton to de new. He don' mix much in sassiety till de bank settlements bin gone done. Skuse me, Sah!—but yo don' happen to know when dat is? It would be a pow'ful heap off de Kernel's mind if it was done. Bein' a high and mighty man in Committees up dah in Sacramento, Sah, I didn't know but what yo might know as it might come befo' yo.'

'I'll see about it,' said Paul, with an odd abstracted smile.

'Shampoo dis mornen', Sah?'

'Nothing more in this line,' said Paul, rising from his chair, 'but something more, perhaps, in the line of your other duties. You're a good barber for the public, George, and I don't take back what I said about your future; but *just now* I think the Colonel wants all your service. He's not at all well. Take this,' he said, putting a twenty-dollar gold piece in the astonished servant's hand, 'and for the next three or four days drop the shop, and under some pretext or another arrange to be with him. That money will cover what you lose here, and as soon as the Colonel's all right again you can come back to work. But are you not afraid of being recognised by someone?'

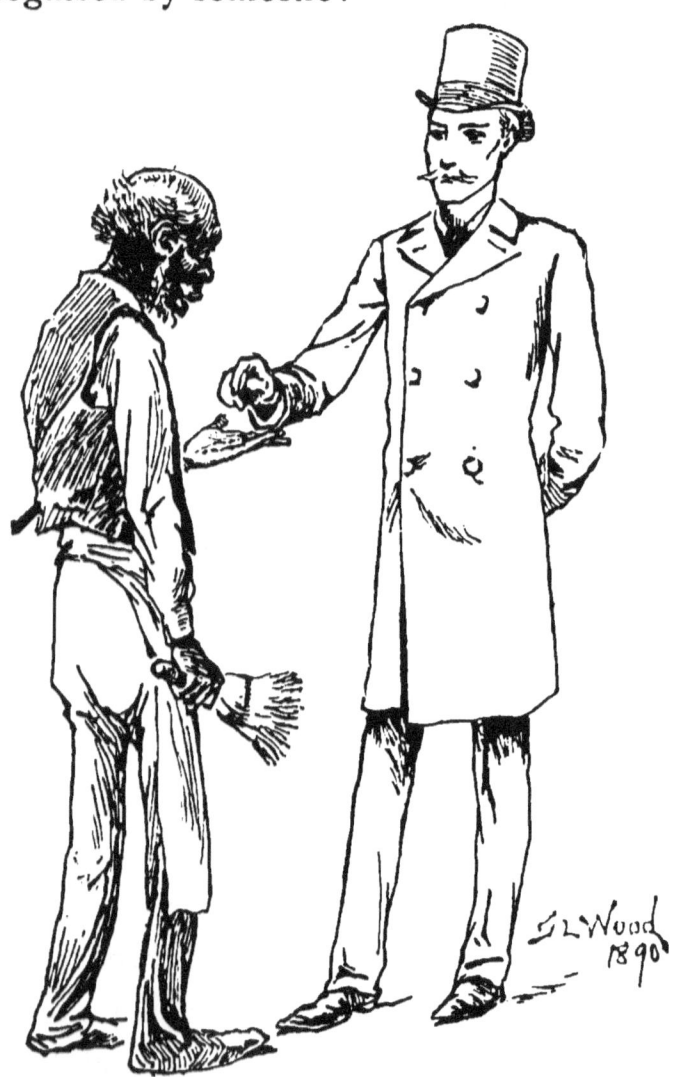

'Take this,' he said

'No, Sah, dat's just it. On'y strangers dat don' know no better come yere.'

'But suppose your master should drop in? It's quite convenient to his rooms.'

'Marse Harry in a barber-shop!' said the old man, with a silent laugh. 'Skuse me, Sah,' he added with an apologetic mixture of respect and dignity, 'but fo' twenty years no man hez touched de Kernel's chin but myself. When Marse Harry hez to go to a barber's shop, it won't make no matter who's dar.'

'Let's hope he will not,' said Paul, gaily; then, anxious to evade the gratitude which since his munificence he had seen beaming in the old negro's eye and evidently trying to find polysyllabic and elevated expression on his lips, he said hurriedly, 'I shall expect to find you with the Colonel when I call again in a day or two,' and smilingly departed.

At the end of two hours George's barber-employer returned to relieve his assistant, and, on receiving from him an account and a certain percentage of the afternoon's fees (minus the gift from Paul), was informed by George that he should pretermit his attendance for a few days. 'Udder private and personal affairs,' explained the old negro, who made no social

'George, don't lie to me, or——'

distinction in his vocabulary, 'peroccupyin' dis niggah's time.' The head barber, unwilling to lose a really good assistant, endeavoured to dissuade him by the offer of increased emolument, but George was firm.

As he entered the sitting-room the Colonel detected his step, and called him in.

'Another time, George, never allow a guest of mine to send away wine. If he don't care for it, put it on the sideboard.'

'Yes, Sah; but as yo didn't like it yo'self, Marse Harry, and de wine was de most 'xpensive quality ob Glencoe'——

'D—n the expense!' He paused, and gazed searchingly at his old retainer.

'George,' he said suddenly, yet in a gentle voice, 'don't lie to me, or'—in a still kinder voice—'I'll flog the black skin off you! Listen to me. *Have* you got any money left?'

''Deed, Sah, dere *is*,' said the negro, earnestly. 'I'll jist fetch it wid de accounts.'

'Hold on! I've been thinking, lying here, that if the Widow Molloy can't pay because she sold out, and that tobacconist is ruined, and we've had to pay the water tax for old Bill Soames, the rent last week don't amount to much, while there's the month's bill for the restaurant and that blank druggist's account for lotions and medicines to come out of it. It strikes me we're pretty near touching bottom. I've everything I want here, but, by God, Sir,

Took from it a striped cotton handkerchief

if I find *you* skimping yourself or lying to me, or borrowing money '——

'Yes, Marse Harry, but the Widow Molloy done gone and paid up dis afernoon. I'll bring de books and money to prove it,' and he hurriedly re-entered the sitting-room.

Then with trembling hands he emptied his pockets on the table, including Paul's gift and the fees he had just received, and opening a desk-drawer took from it a striped cotton handkerchief, such as negro women wear on their heads, containing a small quantity of silver tied up in a hard knot, and a boy's purse. This he emptied on the table with his own money.

They were the only rents of Colonel Henry Pendleton! They were contributed by 'George Washington Thomson'; his wife, otherwise known as 'Aunt Dinah,' washerwoman; and 'Scipio Thomson,' their son, aged fourteen, bootblack. It did not amount to much. But in that happy moisture that dimmed the old man's eyes, God knows it looked large enough.

CHAPTER III

ALTHOUGH the rays of an unclouded sun were hot in the Santa Clara roads and byways, and the dry, bleached dust had become an impalpable powder, the perspiring and parched pedestrian who rashly sought relief in the shade of the wayside oak was speedily chilled to the bone by the north-west trade-winds that on those August afternoons swept through the defiles of the coast range, and even penetrated the pastoral valley of San José. The anomaly of straw hats and overcoats with the occupants of buggies and station wagons was thus accounted for, and even in the sheltered garden of 'El Rosario' two young girls in light summer dresses had thrown wraps over their shoulders as they lounged down a broad rose-alley at

Two young girls in light summer dresses

right angles with the deep long verandah of the *casa*. Yet, in spite of the chill, the old Spanish house and gardens presented a luxurious, almost tropical, picture from the roadside. Banks, beds, and bowers of roses lent their name and colour to the grounds; tree-like clusters of hanging-fuchsias, mound-like masses of variegated verbena, and tangled thickets of ceanothus and spreading heliotrope were set in boundaries of venerable olive-, fig-, and pear-trees. The old house itself, a picturesque relief to the glaring newness of the painted villas along the road, had been tastefully modified to suit the needs and habits of a later civilisation; the galleries of the inner courtyard, or *patio*, had been transferred to the outside walls in the form of deep verandahs, while the old adobe walls themselves were hidden beneath flowing Cape jessamine or bestarred passion vines, and topped by roofs of cylindrical red tiles.

'Miss Yerba!' said a dry, masculine voice from the verandah.

The taller young girl started, and drew herself suddenly behind a large Castilian rose-tree, dragging her companion with her, and putting her finger imperatively upon a pretty but somewhat passionate mouth. The other girl checked a laugh, and remained watching her friend's wickedly levelled brows in amused surprise.

The call was repeated from the verandah. After a moment's pause there was the sound of retreating foot-steps, and all was quiet again.

'Why, for goodness' sake, didn't you answer, Yerba?' asked the shorter girl.

'Oh, I hate him!' responded Yerba. 'He only wanted to bore me with his stupid, formal, sham-parental talk. Because he's my official guardian he thinks it necessary to assume this manner towards me when we meet, and treats me as if I were something between his step-daughter and an almshouse orphan or a police board. It's perfectly ridiculous, for it's only put on while he is in office, and he knows it, and I know it, and I'm tired of making believe. Why, my dear, they change every election; I've had seven of them, all more or less of this kind, since I can remember.'

'But I thought there were two others, dear, that were not official,' said her companion coaxingly.

Yerba sighed. 'No; there was another,

who was president of a bank, but that was also to be official if he died. I used to like him, he seemed to be the only gentleman among them; but it appears that he is dreadfully improper; shoots people now and then for nothing at all, and burst up his bank—and, of course, he's impossible, and, as there's no more bank, when he dies there'll be no more trustee.'

'And there's the third, you know—a stranger, who never appears?' suggested the younger girl.

'And who do you suppose *he* turns out to be? Do you remember that conceited little wretch—that 'Baby Senator,' I think they called him—who was in the parlour of the Golden Gate the other morning surrounded by his idiotic worshippers and toadies and ballot-box stuffers? Well, if you please, *that's* Mr. Paul Hathaway—the Honourable Paul Hathaway, who washed his hands of me, my dear, at the beginning!'

'But really, Yerba, I thought that he looked and acted——'

'You thought of nothing at all, Milly,' returned Yerba, with au hority. 'I tell you he's a mass of conceit. What else could you expect of a Man—toadied and fawned upon to that extent? It made me sick! I could have just shaken them!'

As if to emphasise her statement, she grasped one of the long willowy branches of the enormous rose-bush where she stood, and shook it lightly. The action detached a few of the maturer blossoms, and sent down a shower of faded pink petals on her dark hair and yellow dress. 'I can't bear conceit,' she added.

'Oh, Yerba, just stand as you are! I do wish the girls could see you. You make the *loveliest* picture!'

She certainly did look very pretty as she stood there—a few leaves lodged in her hair, clinging to her dress, and suggesting by reflection the colour that her delicate satin skin would have resented in its own texture. But she turned impatiently away—perhaps not before she had allowed this passing vision to impress the mind of her devoted adherent—and said, 'Come along, or that dreadful man will be out on the verandah again.'

'But, if you dislike him so, why did you

accept the invitation to meet him here at luncheon?' said the curious Milly.

'*I* didn't accept; the Mother Superior did for me, because he's the Mayor of San Francisco visiting your uncle, and she's always anxious to please the powers that be. And I thought he might have some information that I could get out of him. And it was better than being in the convent all day. And I thought I could stand *him* if you were here.'

Milly gratefully accepted this doubtful proof of affection by squeezing her companion's arm. 'And you didn't get any information, dear?'

'Of course not! The idiot knows only the old tradition of his office—that I was a mysterious Trust left in Mayor Hammersley's hands. He actually informed me that "Buena" meant "Good"; that it was likely the name of the captain of some whaler, that put into San Francisco in the early days, whose child I was, and that, if I chose to call myself 'Miss Good," he would allow it, and get a Bill passed in the Legislature to legalise it. Think of it, my dear!—" Miss Good," like one of Mrs. Barbauld's stories, or a moral governess in the "Primary Reader."'

'"Miss Good,"' repeated Milly, innocently. 'Yes, you might put an *e* at the end—G-double-o-d-e. There are Goodes in Philadelphia. And then you won't have to sacrifice that sweet pretty "Yerba," that's so stylish and musical, for you'd still be "Yerba Good." But,' she added, as Yerba made an impatient gesture, 'why do you worry yourself about *that*? You wouldn't keep your own name long, whatever it was. An heiress like you, dear—lovely and accomplished—would have the best names as well as the best men in America to choose from.'

'Now, please, don't repeat that idiot's words. That's what *he* says; that's what they *all* say!' returned Yerba, pettishly. 'One would really think it was necessary for me to get married to become anybody at all, or have any standing whatever. And, whatever you do, don't go talking of me as if I were named after a vegetable. "Yerba Buena" is the name of an island in the bay just off San Francisco. I'm named after that.'

'But I don't see the difference, dear. The island was named after the vine that grows on it.'

'*You* don't see the difference?' said Yerba, darkly. 'Well, *I* do. But what are you looking at?'

Her companion had caught her arm, and was gazing intently at the house.

'Yerba,' she said quickly, 'there's the Mayor, and uncle, and a strange gentleman coming down the walk. They're looking for us. And, as I live, Yerb! the strange gentleman is that young Senator, Mr. Hathaway!'

'Mr. Hathaway? Nonsense!'

'Look for yourself.'

Yerba glanced at the three gentlemen, who, a hundred yards distant, were slowly advancing in the direction of the ceanothus hedge, behind which the girls had instinctively strayed during their conversation.

'What are you going to do?' said Milly, eagerly. 'They're coming straight this way. Shall we stay here and let them pass, or make a run for the house?'

'No,' said Yerba, to Milly's great surprise.

that would look as if we cared. Besides, I
[do]n't know that Mr. Hathaway has come to
[see] *me*. We'll stroll out and meet them
[ac]cidentally.'

Milly was still more astonished. However,
[sh]e said: 'Wait a moment, dear!' and, with
[the] instinctive deftness of her sex, in three
[sm]all tugs and a gentle hitch, shook Yerba's
[go]wn into perfect folds, passed her fingers
[ac]ross her forehead and over her ears, securing,
[ho]wever, with a hairpin on their passage three
[of] the rose petals where they had fallen.
[Th]en, discharging their faces of any previous
[ex]pression, these two charming hypocrites
[sa]lied out innocently into the walk. Nothing
[co]uld be more natural than their manner: if a
[cri]ticism might be ventured upon, it was that
[th]eir elbows were slightly drawn inwards and
[be]fore them, leaving their hands gracefully
[ad]vanced in the line of their figures, an attitude
[ac]cepted throughout the civilised world of
[de]portment as indicating fastidious refinement
[no]t unmingled with permissible hauteur.

The three gentlemen lifted their hats at this

ravishing apparition, and halted. The Mayor advanced with great politeness.

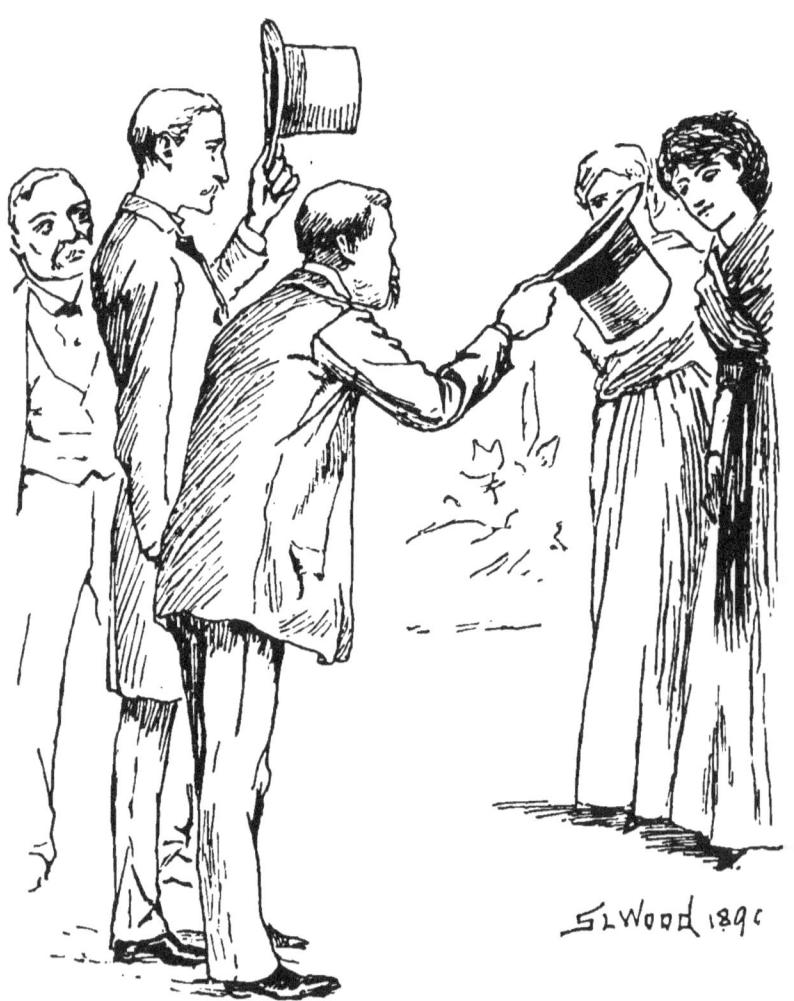

The three gentlemen lifted their hats

'I feared you didn't hear me call you, Miss

Yerba, so we ventured to seek you.' As the two girls exchanged almost infantile glances of surprise, he continued : ' Mr. Paul Hathaway has done us the honour of seeking you here, as he did not find you at the convent. You may have forgotten that Mr. Hathaway is the third one of your trustees.'

'And so inefficient and worthless that I fear he doesn't count,' said Paul, ' but,' raising his eyes to Yerba's, ' I fancy that I have already had the pleasure of seeing you, and, I fear, the mortification of having disturbed you and your friends in the parlour of the Golden Gate Hotel yesterday.'

The two girls looked at each other with the same childlike surprise. Yerba broke the silence by suddenly turning to Milly. ' Certainly, you remember how greatly interested we were in the conversation of a party of gentlemen who were there when we came in. I am afraid our foolish prattle must have disturbed *you.* I know that we were struck with the intelligent and eloquent devotion of your friends.'

' Oh, perfectly,' chimed in the loyal but somewhat infelix Milly ; and it was so kind and thoughtful of Mr. Hathaway to take them away 'as he did.'

'I felt the more embarrassed,' continued Hathaway, smiling, but still critically examining Yerba for an indication of something characteristic, beyond this palpable conventionality, ' as I unfortunately must present my credentials from a gentleman as much of a stranger as myself— Colonel Pendleton.'

The trade-wind was evidently making itself felt even in this pastoral retreat, for the two gentlemen appeared to shrink slightly within themselves, and a chill seemed to have passed over the group. The Mayor coughed. The avuncular Woods gazed abstractedly at a large cactus. Even Paul, prepared by previous experience, stopped short.

'Colonel Pendleton! Oh, do tell me all about him !' flashed out Yerba, suddenly, with clasped hands and eager girlish breath.

Paul cast a quick, grateful glance at the girl. Whether assumed or not, her enthusiastic outburst was effective. The Mayor looked uneasily at Woods, and turned to Paul.

'Ah, yes! You and he were original co-trustees. I believe Pendleton is in reduced circumstances. Never quite got over that bank trouble.'

'That is only a question of legislative investigation and relief,' said Paul, lightly, yet with purposely vague official mystery of manner. Then, turning quickly to Yerba, as if replying to the only real question at issue, he continued pointedly, 'I am sorry to say the Colonel's health is so poor that it keeps him quite a recluse. I have a letter from him and a message for you.' His bright eyes added plainly—'as soon as we can get rid of those people.'

'Then you think that a Bill '——began the Mayor, eagerly.

'I think, my dear Sir,' said Paul, plaintively, 'that I and my friends have already tried the patience of these two young ladies quite enough yesterday with politics and law-making. I have to catch the six-o'clock train to San Francisco this evening, and have already lost the time I hoped to spend with Miss Yerba by missing her at the convent. Let me stroll on here, if you like, and if I venture to monopolise the attention of this young lady for half an hour, you, my dear Mr. Mayor, who have more frequent access to her, I know will not begrudge it to me.'

He placed himself beside Yerba and Milly, and began an entertaining, although, I fear, slightly exaggerated account of his reception by the Lady Superior, and her evident doubts of his identity with the trustee mentioned in Pendleton's letter of introduction. 'I confess she frightened me,' he continued, 'when she remarked that, according to my statement, I could have been only eighteen years old when I became your guardian, and as much in want of one as you were. I think that only her belief that Mr. Woods and the Mayor would detect me as an impostor provoked her at last to tell me your whereabouts.'

'But why *did* they ever make you a trustee, for goodness' sake?' said Milly, naïvely. 'Was there no one grown up at that time that they could have called upon?'

'Those were the *early* days of California,' responded Paul, with great gravity, although he was conscious that Yerba was regarding him narrowly, 'and I probably looked older and more intelligent than I really was. For, candidly,' with the consciousness of Yerba's eyes still upon him, 'I remember very little about it. I dare say I was selected, as you kindly suggest, "for goodness' sake."'

'After all,' said the volatile Milly, who seemed inclined, as chaperon, to direct the conversation, 'there was something pretty and romantic about it. You two poor young things taking care of each other, for, of course, there were no women here in those days.'

'Of course there *were* women here,' interrupted Yerba, quickly, with a half-meaning, half-interrogative glance at Paul that made him instinctively uneasy. 'You later comers'—to Milly—'always seem to think that there was nothing here before you!' She paused, and then added, with a naïve mixture of reproach and coquetry that was as charming as it was unexpected, 'As to taking care of each other, Mr. Hathaway very quickly got rid of me, I believe.'

'But I left you in better hands, Miss Yerba; and let me thank you now,' he added in a lower tone, 'for recognising it as you did a moment ago. I'm glad that you instinctively liked Colonel Pendleton. Had you known him better, you would have seen how truthful that instinct was. His chief fault in the eyes of our worthy friends is that he reminds them of a great deal they can't perpetuate and much they would like to forget.' He checked himself abruptly. 'But here is your letter,' he resumed, drawing Colonel Pendleton's missive from his pocket; 'perhaps you would like to read it now, in case you have any message to return by me. Miss Woods and I will excuse you.'

They had reached the end of the rose-alley, where a summer-house that was in itself a rose-bower partly disclosed itself. The other gentlemen had lagged behind. 'I will amuse *myself*, and console your other guardian, dear,' said the vivacious Milly, with a rapid exchange of glances with Yerba, 'until this horrid business is over. Besides,' she added with cheerful vagueness, 'after so long a separation you must have a great deal to say to each other.'

Paul smiled as she rustled away, and Yerba, entering the summer-house, sat down and opened the letter. The young man remained leaning against the rustic archway, occasionally glancing at her and at the moving figures in the gardens. He was conscious of an odd excitement which he could trace to no particular cause. It was true that he had been annoyed at not finding the young girl at the convent, and at having to justify himself to the Lady Superior for what he conceived to be an act of gratuitous kindness; nor was he blind to the fact that his persistence in following her was more an act of aggression against the enemies of Pendleton than of concern for Yerba. She was certainly pretty; but he could not remember her mother sufficiently to trace any likeness, and he had never admired the mother's pronounced beauty. She had flashed out for an instant into what seemed originality and feeling. But it had passed, and she had asked no further questions in regard to the Colonel.

She had hurriedly skimmed through the letter, which seemed to be composed of certain figures and accounts. 'I suppose it's all right,' she said: 'at least, you can say so if he asks you. It's only an explanation why he has transferred my money from the bank to Rothschild's agent years ago. I don't see why it should interest me *now*.'

'I suppose it is all right,' she said

Paul made no doubt that it was the same

transfer that had shipwrecked the Colonel's fortune and alienated his friends, and could not help replying somewhat pointedly, 'But I think it should, Miss Yerba. I don't know what the Colonel explained to you—doubtless, not the whole truth, for he is not a man to praise himself; but, the fact is, the bank was in difficulties at the time of that transfer, and, to make it, he sacrificed his personal fortune, and, I think, awakened some of that ill-feeling you have just noticed.' He checked himself too late: he had again lost not only his tact and self-control, but had nearly betrayed himself. He was surprised that the girl's justifiable ignorance should have irritated him. Yet she had evidently not noticed, or misunderstood it, for she said, with a certain precision that was almost studied—

'Yes, I suppose it would have been a terrible thing to him to have been suspected of misappropriating a Trust confided to him by parties who had already paid him the high compliment of confiding to his care a secret and a fortune.'

Paul glanced at her quickly with astonishment. Was this ignorance, or suspicion? Her manner, however, suddenly changed, with the charming capriciousness of youth and conscious beauty. 'He speaks of you in this letter,' she said, letting her dark eyes rest on him provokingly.

'That accounts for your lack of interest, then,' said Paul, gaily, relieved to turn a conversation fraught with so much danger.

'But he speaks very flatteringly,' she went on. 'He seems to be another one of your admirers. I'm sure, Mr. Hathaway, after that scene in the hotel parlour yesterday, *you*, at least, cannot complain of having been misrepresented before *me*. To tell you the truth, I think I hated you a little for it.'

'You were quite right,' returned Paul. 'I must have been insufferable! And I admit that I was slightly piqued against *you* for the idolatries showered upon you at the same moment by your friends.'

Usually, when two young people have reached the point of confidingly exchanging their first impressions of each other, some progress has been made in first acquaintance. But it did not strike Paul in that way, and Yerba's next remark was discouraging.

'But I'm rather disappointed, for all that Colonel Pendleton tells me you know nothing of my family or of the secret.'

Paul was this time quite prepared, and withstood the girl's scrutiny calmly. 'Do you think,' he asked lightly, 'that even *he* knows?'

'Of course he does,' she returned quickly. 'Do you suppose he would have taken all that trouble you have just talked about if he didn't know it? And feared the consequences, perhaps?' she added, with a slight return of her previous expressive manner.

Again Paul was puzzled and irritated, he knew not why. But he only said pleasantly, 'I differ from you there. I am afraid that such a thing as fear never entered into Colonel Pendleton's calculations on any subject. I think he would act the same towards the highest and the lowest, the powerful or the most weak.' As she glanced at him quickly and mischievously, he added, 'I am quite willing to believe that his knowledge of you made his duty pleasanter.'

He was again quite sincere, and his slight sympathy had that irresistible quality of tone and look which made him so dangerous. For he was struck with the pretty soothed self-complacency that had shone in her face since he had spoken of Pendleton's equal disinterestedness. It seemed, too, as if what he had taken for passion or petulance in her manner had been only a resistance to some continual aggression of condition. With that remainder held in check, a certain latent nobility was apparent, as of her true self. In this moment of pleased abstraction she had drawn through the latticework of one of the windows a spray of roses still clinging to the vine, and, with her graceful head a little on one side, was softly caressing her cheek with it. She certainly was very pretty. From the crown of her dark little head to the narrow rosetted slipper that had been idly tapping the ground, but now seemed to tread it more proudly, with arched instep and small ankle, she was pleasant to look upon.

'But you surely have something else to think about, Miss Yerba?' said the young man, with conviction. 'In a few months you will be of age, and rid of those dreadfully stupid guardians ; with your——'

The loosened rose-spray flew from her hand out of the window as she made a gesture, half real, half assumed, of imploring supplication. 'Oh, please, Mr. Hathaway, for Heaven's sake don't *you* begin too! You are going to say that, with my wealth, my accomplishments, my beauty, my friends, what more can I want? What do I care about a secret that can neither add to them nor take them away? Yes, you were! It's the regular thing to say—everybody says it. Why, I should have thought ' the youngest senator' could afford to have been more original.'

'I plead guilty to *all* the weaknesses of humanity,' said Paul, warmly, again beginning to believe that he had been most unjust to her independence.

'Well, I forgive you, because you have forgotten to say that, if I don't like the name of Yerba Buena, I could *so* easily change that too.'

'But you *do* like it,' said Paul, touched with this first hearing of her name in her own musical accents, 'or would like it if you heard yourself pronounce it.' It suddenly recurred to him, with a strange thrill of pleasure, that he himself had given it to her. It was as if he had created some musical instrument to which she had just given voice. In his enthusiasm he had thrown himself on the bench beside her in an attitude that, I fear, was not as dignified as became his elderly office.

'But you don't think that is my *name*,' said the girl, quickly.

'I beg your pardon?' said Paul, hesitatingly.

'You don't think that anybody would have been so utterly idiotic as to call me after a ground-vine—a vegetable?' she continued petulantly.

'Eh?' stammered Paul.

'A name that could be so easily translated, she went on, half-scornfully, 'and, when translated, was no possible title for anybody? Think of it—Miss Good Herb! It is too ridiculous for anything.'

Paul was not usually wanting in self-possession in an emergency, or in skill to meet attack. But he was so convinced of the truth of the girl's accusation, and now recalled so vividly his own consternation on hearing the result of his youthful and romantic sponsorship for the first time from Pendleton, that he was struck with confusion.

'But what do you suppose it was intended for?' he said at last, vaguely. 'It was certainly 'Yerba Buena' in the Trust. At least, I suppose so,' he corrected himself hurriedly.

'It is only a supposition,' she said quietly, 'for you know it cannot be proved. The Trust was never recorded, and the only copy could not be found among Mr. Hammersley's papers. It is only part of the name, of which the first is lost.'

'Part of the name?' repeated Paul, uneasily.

'Part of it. It is a corruption of *de la Yerba Buena*—of the Yerba Buena—and refers to the island of Yerba Buena in the bay, and not to the plant. That island was part of the property of my family—the Arguellos—you will find it so recorded in the Spanish grants. My name is Arguello de la Yerba Buena.

It is impossible to describe the timid yet

triumphant, the half-appealing yet complacent, conviction of the girl's utterance. A moment before, Paul would have believed it impossible for him to have kept his gravity and his respect for his companion under this egregious illusion. But he kept both. For a sudden conviction that she suspected the truth, and had taken this audacious and original plan of crushing it, overpowered all other sense. The Arguellos, it flashed upon him, were an old Spanish family, former owners of Yerba Buena Island, who had in the last years become extinct. There had been a story that one of them had eloped with an American ship captain's wife at Monterey. The legendary history of early Spanish California was filled with more remarkable incidents, corroborated with little difficulty from Spanish authorities, who, it was alleged, lent themselves readily to any fabrication or forgery. There was no racial pride; on the contrary, they had shown an eager alacrity to ally themselves with their conquerors. The friends of the Arguellos would be proud to recognise and remember in the American heiress the descendant of their countrymen.

All this passed rapidly through his mind after the first moment of surprise; all this must have been the deliberate reasoning of this girl of seventeen, whose dark eyes were bent upon him. Whether she was seeking corroboration or complicity he could not tell.

'Have you found this out yourself?' he asked, after a pause.

'Yes. One of my friends at the convent was Josita Castro; she knew all the history of the Arguellos. She is perfectly satisfied.'

For an instant Paul wondered if it was a joint conception of the two school-girls. But, on reflection, he was persuaded that Yerba would commit herself to no accomplice—of her own sex. She might have dominated the girl, and would make her a firm partisan, while the girl would be convinced of it herself, and believe herself a free agent. He had had such experience with men himself.

'But why have you not spoken of it before—and to Colonel Pendleton?'

'He did not choose to tell *me*,' said Yerba, with feminine dexterity. 'I have preferred to keep it myself a secret till I am of age.'

When Colonel Pendleton and some of the other trustees have no right to say anything, thought Paul quickly. She had evidently trusted *him*. Yet, fascinated as he had been by her audacity, he did not know whether to be pleased, or the reverse. He would have preferred to be placed on an equal footing with Josita Castro. She anticipated his thoughts by saying, with half-raised eyelids—

'What do *you* think of it?'

'It seems to be so natural and obvious an explanation of the mystery that I only wonder it was not thought of before,' said Paul, with that perfect sincerity that made his sympathy so effective.

'You see'—still under her pretty eyelids, and the tender promise of a smile parting her little mouth—'I'm believing that you tell the truth when you say you don't know anything about it.'

It was a desperate moment with Paul, but his sympathetic instincts, and possibly his luck, triumphed. His momentary hesitation easily simulated the caution of a conscientious man; his knit eyebrows and bright eyes, lowered in an effort of memory, did the rest. 'I remember it all so indistinctly,' he said, with literal truthfulness; 'there was a veiled lady present, tall and dark, to whom Mayor Hammersley and the Colonel showed a singular, and it struck me, as an almost superstitious, respect. I remember now, distinctly, I was impressed with the reverential way they both accompanied her to the door at the end of the interview.' He raised his eyes slightly; the young girl's red lips were parted; that illumination of the skin, which was her nearest approach to colour, had quite transfigured her face. He felt, suddenly, that she believed it, yet he had no sense of remorse. He half-believed it himself; at least, he remembered the nobility of the mother's self-renunciation and its effect upon the two men. Why should not the daughter preserve this truthful picture of the mother's momentary exaltation? Which was the most truthful— that, or the degrading facts? 'You speak of a secret,' he added. 'I can remember little more than that the Mayor asked me to forget, from that moment, the whole occurrence. I did not know at the time how completely I should fulfil his request. You must remember, Miss Yerba, as your Lady Superior has, that I was absurdly young at the time. I don't know but that I may have thought, in my youthful inexperience, that this sort of thing was of common occurrence. And then, I had my own future to make—and youth is brutally selfish. I was quite friendless and unknown when I left San Francisco for the mines, at the time you entered the convent as Yerba Buena.'

She smiled, and made a slight impulsive gesture, as if she would have drawn nearer to him, but checked herself, still smiling, and without embarrassment. It may have been a movement of youthful *camaraderie*, and that occasional maternal rather than sisterly instinct which sometimes influences a young girl's masculine friendship, and elevates the favoured friend to the plane of the doll she has outgrown. As he turned towards her, however, she rose, shook out her yellow dress, and said with pretty petulance—

'Then you must go so soon—and this your first and last visit as my guardian?'

'No one could regret that more than I,' looking at her with undefined meaning.

'Yes,' she said, with a tantalising coquetry that might have suggested an underlying seriousness, 'I think you *have* lost a good deal. Perhaps, so have I. We might have been good friends in all these years. But that is past.'

'Why? Surely, I hope, my shortcomings with Miss Yerba Buena will not be remembered by Miss Arguello?' said Paul, earnestly.

'Ah! *She* may be a very different person.'

'I hope not,' said the young man, warmly. 'But *how* different?'

'Well, she may not put herself in the way of receiving such point-blank compliments as that,' said the young girl, demurely.

'Not from her guardian?'

'She will have no guardian then.' She said this gravely, but almost at the same moment turned and sat down again, throwing her linked hands over her knee, and looked at him mischievously. 'You see what you have lost, Sir.'

'I see,' said Paul, but with all the gravity that she had dropped.

'No; but you don't see all. I had no brother—no friend. You might have been both. You might have made me what you liked. You might have educated me far better than these teachers, or, at least, given me some pride in my studies. There were so many things I wanted to know that they couldn't teach me; so many times I wanted advice from someone that I could trust. Colonel Pendleton was very good to me when he came; he always treated me like a princess even when I wore short frocks. It was his manner that first made me think he knew my family; but I never felt as if I could tell him anything, and I don't think, with all his chivalrous respect, he ever understood me. As to the others—the Mayors—well, you may judge from Mr. Henderson. It is a wonder that I did not run away or do something desperate. Now, are you not a *little* sorry?'

Her voice, which had as many capricious changes as her manner, had been alternately coquettish, petulant, and serious, had now become playful again. But, like the rest of her sex, she was evidently more alert to her surroundings at such a moment than her companion, for before he could make any reply she said, without apparently looking, 'But there is a deputation coming for you, Mr. Hathaway. You see, the case is hopeless. You never would be able to give to one what is claimed by the many.'

Paul glanced down the rose-alley, and saw that the deputation in question was composed of the Mayor, Mr. Woods, a thin, delicate-looking woman—evidently Mrs. Woods—and Milly. The latter managed to reach the summer-house first, with apparently youthful alacrity, but really to exchange, in a single glance, some mysterious feminine signal with Yerba. Then she said with breathless infelicity—

'Before you two get bored with each other now, I must tell you there's a chance of you having more time. Aunty has promised to send off a note excusing you to the Reverend Mother, if she can persuade Mr. Hathaway to stay over to-night. But here they are. [To Yerba] Aunty is most anxious, and won't hear of his going.'

Indeed, it seemed as if Mrs. Woods was, after a refined fashion, most concerned that a distinguished visitor like Mr. Hathaway should have to use her house as a mere accidental meeting-place with his ward, without deigning to accept her hospitality. She was reinforced by Mr. Woods, who enunciated the same idea with more masculine vigour; and by the Mayor, who expressed his conviction that a slight of this kind to Rosario would be felt in the Santa Clara valley. 'After dinner, my dear Hathaway,' concluded Mr. Woods, 'a few of our neighbours may drop in, who would be glad to shake you by the hand—no formal meeting, my boy—but, hang it! *they* expect it.'

Paul looked around for Yerba. There was really no reason why he shouldn't accept, although an hour ago the idea had never entered his mind. Yet, if he did, he would like the girl to know that it was for *her* sake. Unfortunately, far from exhibiting any concern in the matter, she seemed to be preoccupied with Milly, and only the charming back of her head was visible behind Mrs. Woods. He accepted, however, with a hesitation that took some of the graciousness from his yielding, and a sense that he was giving a strange importance to a trivial circumstance.

The necessity of attaching himself to his hostess, and making a more extended tour of the grounds, for a while diverted him from an uneasy consideration of his past interview. Mrs. Woods had known Yerba through the school friendship of Milly, and, as far as the religious rules of the convent would allow, had always been delighted to show her any hospitality. She was a beautiful girl—did not Mr. Hathaway think so?—and a girl of great character. It was a pity, of course, that she had never known a mother's care, and that the present routine of a boarding-school had usurped the tender influences of home. She believed, too, that the singular rotation of guardianship had left the girl practically without a counselling friend to rely upon, except, perhaps, Colonel Pendleton; and while she, Mrs. Woods, did not for a moment doubt that the Colonel might be a good friend and a pleasant companion of *men*, really he, Mr. Hathaway, must admit that, with his reputation and habits, he was hardly a fit associate for a young lady. Indeed, Mr. Woods would never have allowed Milly to invite Yerba here if Colonel Pendleton was to have been her escort. Of course, the poor girl could not choose her own guardian, but Mr. Woods said *he* had a right to choose who should be his niece's company. Perhaps Mr. Woods was prejudiced—most men were—yet surely Mr. Hathaway, although a loyal friend of Colonel Pendleton's, must admit that when it was an open scandal that the Colonel had fought a duel about a notoriously common woman, and even blasphemously defended her before a party of gentlemen, it was high time, as Mr. Woods said, that he should be remanded to their company exclusively. No; Mrs. Woods could not admit that this was owing to the injustice of her own sex! Men are really the ones who make the fuss over those things, just as they, as Mr. Hathaway well knew, made the laws! No; it was a great pity, as she and her husband had just agreed, that Mr. Hathaway, of all the guardians, could not have been always the help and counsellor—in fact, the elder brother—of poor Yerba! Paul was conscious that he winced slightly, consistently and conscientiously, at the recollection of certain passages of his youth; inconsistently and meanly, at this suggestion of a joint relationship with Yerba's mother.

'I think, too,' continued Mrs. Woods, 'she has worried foolishly about this ridiculous mystery of her parentage—as if it could make the slightest difference to a girl with a quarter of a million, or as if that didn't show quite conclusively that she *was* somebody!'

'Certainly,' said Paul, quickly, with a relief that he nevertheless felt was ridiculous.

'And, of course, I dare say it will all come out when she is of age. I suppose you know if any of the family are still living?'

'I really do not.'

'I beg your pardon,' said Mrs. Woods, with a smile, 'I forgot it's a profound secret until then. But here we are at the house; I see the girls have walked over to our neighbours'. Perhaps you would like to have a few moments to yourself before you dress for dinner, and your portmanteau, which has been sent for, comes from your hotel. You must be tired of seeing so many people.'

Paul was glad to accept any excuse for being alone, and, thanking his hostess, followed a servant to his room—a low-ceilinged but luxuriously furnished apartment on the first floor. Here he threw himself on a cushioned lounge that filled the angle of the deep embrasure—the thickness of the old adobe walls— that formed a part of the wooden-latticed window. A Cape jessamine climbing beside it filled the room with its subtle, intoxicating perfume. It was so strong, and he felt himself so irresistibly overpowered and impelled towards a merely idle reverie, that, in order to think more clearly and shut out some strange and unreasoning enthralment of his senses, he rose and sharply closed the window. Then he sat down and reflected.

What was he doing here? and what was the meaning of all this? He had come simply to fulfil a duty to his past, and please a helpless and misunderstood old acquaintance. He had performed that duty. But he had incidentally learned a certain fact that might be important to this friend, and clearly his duty was simply to go back and report it. He would gain

He sharply closed the window

nothing more in the way of corroboration of it by staying now, if further corroboration were required. Colonel Pendleton had already been uselessly and absurdly perplexed about the possible discovery of the girl's parentage, and its effect upon her fortunes and herself. She had just settled that of her own accord, and, without committing herself or others, had suggested a really sensible plan by which all trouble would be avoided in future. That was the common-sense way of looking at it. He would lay the plan before the Colonel, have him judge of its expediency and its ethics— and even the question whether she already knew the real truth, or was self deceived. That done, he would return to his own affairs in Sacramento. There was nothing difficult in this, or that need worry him, only he could have done it just as well an hour ago.

He opened the window again. The scent of the jessamine came in as before, but mingled with the cooler breath of the roses. There was nothing intoxicating or unreal in it now; rather it seemed a gentle aromatic stimulant— of thought. Long shadows of unseen poplars beyond barred the garden lanes and alleys with bands of black and yellow. A slanting pencil of sunshine through the trees was for a moment focussed on a bed of waxen callas before a hedge of ceanothus, and struck into dazzling relief the cold white chalices of the flowers and the vivid shining green of their background. Presently it slid beyond to a tiny fountain, before invisible, and wrought a blinding miracle out of its flashing and leaping spray. Yet even as he gazed the fountain seemed to vanish slowly, the sunbeam slipped on, and beyond it moved the shimmer of white and yellow dresses. It was Yerba and Milly returning to the house. Well, he would not interrupt his reflections by idly watching them; he would, probably, see a great deal of Yerba that evening, and by that time he would have come to some conclusion in regard to her.

But he had not taken into consideration her voice, which, always musical in its Southern intonation and quite audible in the quiet garden, struck him now as being full of joyous sweetness. Well, she was certainly very happy—or very thoughtless. She was actually romping with Milly, and was now evidently being chased down the rose-alley by that volatile young woman. Then these swift Camillas apparently neared the house, there was the rapid rustle of skirts, the skurrying of little feet on the verandah, a stumble, a mouse-like shriek from Milly, and *her* voice, exhausted, dying, happy, broken with half-hushed laughter, rose to him on the breath of the jessamine and rose.

Surely she *was* a child, and, if a child, how he had misjudged her! What if all that he had believed was mature deliberation was only the innocent imaginings of a romantic girl, all that he had taken seriously only a schoolgirl's foolish dream! Instead of combating it, instead of reasoning with her, instead of trying to interest her in other things, he had even helped on her illusions. He had treated her as if the taint of her mother's worldliness and knowledge of evil was in her pure young flesh. He had recognised her as the daughter of an adventuress, and not as his ward, appealing to his chivalry through her very ignorance—it might be her very childish vanity. He had brought to a question of tender and pathetic interest only his selfish opinion of the world and the weaknesses of mankind. The blood came to his cheeks—with all his experienced self-control, he had not lost the youthful trick of blushing—and he turned away from the window as if it had breathed a reproach.

But ought he have even contented himself with destroying her illusions—ought he not have gone further and told her the whole truth? Ought he not first have won her confidence—he remembered bitterly, now, how she had intimated that she had no one to confide in—and, after revealing her mother's history, have still pledged himself to keep the secret from all others, and assisted her in her plan? It would not have altered the state of affairs, except so far as she was concerned : they could have combined together, his ready wit would have helped him, and his sympathy would have sustained her; but——

How and in what way could he have told her? Leaving out the delicate and difficult periphrase by which her mother's shame would have to be explained to an innocent schoolgirl —what right could he have assumed to tell it? As the guardian who had never counselled or protected her? As an acquaintance of hardly an hour ago? Who would have such a right?

A lover—on whose lips it would only seem a tacit appeal to her gratitude or her fears, and whom no sensitive girl could accept thereafter? No. A husband? Yes! He remembered with a sudden start what Pendleton had said to him. Good heavens! Had Pendleton that idea in his mind? And yet—it seemed the only solution.

A knock at his door was followed by the appearance of Mr. Woods. Mr. Hathaway's portmanteau had come, and Mrs. Woods had sent a message, saying that in view of the limited time that Mr. Hathaway would have with his ward, Mrs. Woods would forego her right to keep him at her side at dinner, and yield her place to Yerba. Paul thanked him with a grave inward smile. What if he made his dramatic disclosure to her confidentially over the soup and fish? Yet, in his constantly recurring conviction of the girl's independence, he made no doubt she would have met his brutality with unflinching pride and self-possession. He began to dress slowly, at times almost forgetting himself in a new kind of pleasant apathy, which he attributed to the odour of the flowers, and the softer hush of twilight that had come on with the dying away of the trade winds, and the restful spice of the bay-trees near his window. He presently found himself not so much thinking of Yerba as *seeing* her. A picture of her in the summer-house caressing her cheek with the roses seemed to stand out from the shadows of the blank wall opposite him. When he passed into the dressing-room beyond, it was not his own face he saw in the glass, but hers. It was with a start, as if he had heard *her* voice, that he found upon his dressing-table a small vase containing a flower for his coat, with the pencilled words on a card in a schoolgirl's hand, 'From Yerba, with thanks for staying.' It must have been placed there by a servant while he was musing at the window.

Half a dozen people were already in the drawing-room when Paul descended. It appeared that Mr. Woods had invited certain of his neighbours—among them a Judge Baker and his wife, and Don Cæsar Briones, of the adjacent Rancho of Los Pajaros, and his sister, the Doña Anna. Milly and Yerba had not yet appeared. Don Cæsar, a young man of a toreador build, roundly bland in face and

A card in a schoolgirl's hand

murky in eye, seemed to notice their absence, and kept his glances towards the door, while

Paul engaged in conversation with Doña Anna —if that word could convey an impression of a conventionality which that good-humoured young lady converted into an animated flirtation at the second sentence with a single glance and two shakes of her fan. And then Milly fluttered in—a vision of schoolgirl freshness and white tulle, and a moment later—with a pause of expectation—a tall, graceful figure, that at first Paul scarcely recognised.

It is a popular conceit of our sex that we are superior to any effect of feminine adornment, and that a pretty girl is equally pretty in the simplest frock. Yet there was not a man in the room who did not believe that Yerba in her present attire was not only far prettier than before, but that she indicated a new and more delicate form of beauty. It was not the mere revelation of contour and colour of an ordinary *décolleté* dress, it was a perfect presentment of pure symmetry and carriage. In this black grenadine dress, trimmed with jet, not only was the delicate satin sheen of her skin made clearer by contrast, but she looked every inch her full height, with an ideal exaltation of breeding and culture. She wore no jewellery except a small necklace of pearls—so small it might have been a child's—that fitted her slender throat so tightly that it could scarcely be told from the flesh that it clasped. Paul did not know that it was the gift of the mother to the child that she had forsworn only a few weeks before she parted from her for ever; but he had a vague feeling that, in that sable dress that seemed like mourning, she walked at the funeral of her mother's past. A few white flowers in her corsage, the companions of the solitary one in his button-hole, were the only relief.

Their eyes met for a single moment, the look of admiration in Paul's being answered by the naïve consciousness in Yerba's of a woman looking her best; but the next moment she appeared preoccupied with the others, and the eager advances of Don Cæsar.

'Your brother seems to admire Miss Yerba,' said Paul.

'Ah, ye—es,' returned Doña Anna. 'And you?'

'Oh!' said Paul, gaily. '*I*? *I* am her guardian—with me it is simple egotism, you know.'

'Ah!' returned the arch Doña Anna, 'you are then already *so* certain of her? Good! I shall warn him.'

A precaution that did seem necessary; as later, when Paul, at a signal from his hostess, offered his arm to Yerba, the young Spaniard regarded him with a look of startled curiosity.

'I thank you for selecting me to wear your colours,' said Paul, with a glance at the flowers in her corsage, as they sat at table, 'and I think I deserve them, since, but for you, I should be on my way to San Francisco at this moment. Shall I have an opportunity of talking to you a few moments later in the evening?' he added, in a lower tone.

'Why not now?' returned Yerba, mischievously. 'We are set here expressly for that purpose.'

'Surely not to talk of our own business—I should say, of our *family* affairs,' said Paul, looking at her with equal playfulness; 'though I believe your friend Don Cæsar, opposite, would be more pleased if he were sure that was all we did.'

'And you think his sister would share in

that pleasure,' retorted Yerba. 'I warn you, Mr. Hathaway, that you have been quite justifying the Reverend Mother's doubts about your venerable pretensions. Everybody is staring at you now.'

Paul looked up mechanically. It was true. Whether from some occult sympathy, from a human tendency to admire obvious fitness and symmetry, or the innocent love with which the world regards youthful lovers, they were all observing Yerba and himself with undisguised attention. A good talker, he quickly led the conversation to other topics. It was then that he discovered that Yerba was not only accomplished, but that this convent-bred girl had acquired a singular breadth of knowledge apart from the ordinary routine of the school curriculum. She spoke and thought with independent perceptions and clearness, yet without the tactlessness and masculine abruptness that is apt to detract from feminine originality of reflection. By some tacit understanding that had the charm of mutual confidence they both exerted themselves to please the company rather than each other, and Paul, in the interchange of

llies with Doña Anna, had a certain pleasure
 hearing Yerba converse in Spanish with Don
æsar. But in a few moments he observed,
ith some uneasiness, that they were talking
 the old Spanish occupation, and presently
 the old Spanish families. Would she pre-
aturely expose an ignorance that might be
:reafter remembered against her, or invite
•me dreadful genealogical reminiscence that
ould destroy her hopes and raze her Spanish
stles? Or was she simply collecting informa-
ɔn? He admired the dexterity with which,
ithout committing herself, she made Don
æsar openly and even confidentially communi-
tive. And yet he was on thorns: at times it
:emed as if he himself were playing a part in
is imposture of Yerba's. He was aware that
s wandering attention was noticed by the
iick-witted Doña Anna, when he regained his
·lf-possession by what appeared to be a happy
version. It was the voice of Mrs. Judge
aker calling across the table to Yerba. By
ιe of the peculiar accidents of general con-
rsation, it was the one apparently trivial re-
ark that in a pause challenged the ears of all

'We were admiring your necklace, Miss Yerba.'

Every eye was turned upon the slender throat of the handsome girl. The excuse was so natural.

Yerba put her hand to her neck with a smile. 'You are joking, Mrs. Baker. I know it is ridiculously small, but it is a child's necklace, and I wear it because it was a gift from my mother.'

Paul's heart sank again with consternation. It was the first time that he had heard the girl distinctly connect herself with her actual mother, and for an instant he felt as startled as if the forgotten Outcast herself had returned and taken a seat at the board.

'I told you it couldn't be so?' said Mrs. Baker, turning to her husband.

Everybody naturally looked inquiringly upon the couple, and Mrs. Baker explained with a smile: 'Bob thinks he's seen it before; men are so obstinate.'

'Pardon me, Miss Yerba,' said the Judge blandly, 'would you mind showing it to me, if it is not too much trouble?'

'Not at all,' said Yerba, smiling, and detaching the circlet from her neck. 'I'm afraid you'll find it rather old-fashioned.'

'That's just what I hope to find it,' said Judge Baker, with a triumphant glance at his wife. 'It was eight years ago when I saw it in Tucker's jewellery shop. I wanted to buy it for my little Minnie, but as the price was steep I hesitated, and when I did make up my mind he had disposed of it to another customer. Yes,' he added, examining the necklace that Yerba had handed to him, 'I am certain it is the same; it was unique, like this. Odd, isn't it?'

Everybody said it *was* odd, and looked upon the occurrence with that unreasoning satisfaction with which average humanity receives the most trivial and unmeaning coincidences. It was left to Don Cæsar to give it a gallant application.

'I have not-a the pleasure of knowing-a the Miss Minnie, but the jewellery, when she arrives, to the throat-a of Miss Yerba, she has not lost the value—the beauty—the charm.'

'No,' said Woods, cheerily. 'The fact is, Baker, you were too slow. Miss Yerba's folks gobbled up the necklace while you were thinking. You were a new comer. Old 'forty-niners' did not hesitate over a thing they wanted.

'You never knew who was your successful rival, eh?' said Doña Anna, turning to Judge Baker with a curious glance at Paul's pale face in passing.

'No,' said Baker, 'but'—— he stopped with a hesitating laugh and some little confusion. 'No, I've mixed it up with something else. It's so long ago. 'I never knew, or if I did I've forgotten. But the necklace I remember.' He handed it back to Yerba with a bow, and the incident ended.

Paul had not looked at Yerba during this conversation, an unreasoning instinct that he might confuse her, an equally unreasoning dread that he might see her confused by others, possessing him. And when he did glance at her calm, untroubled face, that seemed only a little surprised at his own singular coldness, he was by no means relieved. He was only convinced of one thing. In the last five minutes he had settled upon the irrevocable determination that his present relations with the girl could exist no longer. He must either tell her everything, or see her no more. There was no middle course. She was on the brink of an exposure at any moment, either through her ignorance or her unhappy pretension. In his intolerable position, he was equally unable to contemplate her peril, accept her defence, or himself defend her.

As if, with some feminine instinct, she had attributed his silence to some jealousy of Don Cæsar's attentions, she more than once turned from the Spaniard to Paul with an assuring smile. In his anxiety, he half-accepted the rather humiliating suggestion, and managed to say to her, in a lower tone—

'On this last visit of your American guardian, one would think, you need not already anticipate your Spanish relations.'

He was thrilled with the mischievous yet faintly tender pleasure that sparkled in her eyes as she said—

'You forget it is my American guardian's *first* visit, as well as his last.'

'And as your guardian,' he went on, with half-veiled seriousness, 'I protest against your

K

allowing your treasures, the property of the Trust,' he gazed directly into her beautiful eyes, 'being handled and commented upon by everybody.'

When the ladies had left the table, he was, for a moment, relieved. But only for a moment. Judge Baker drew his chair beside Paul's, and taking his cigar from his lips, said, with a perfunctory laugh—

'I say, Hathaway, I pulled up just in time to save myself from making an awful speech, just now, to your ward.'

Paul looked at him with cold curiosity.

'Yes. Gad! Do you know *who* was my rival in that necklace transaction?'

'No,' said Paul, with frigid carelessness.

'Why, Kate Howard! Fact, Sir. She bought it right under my nose—and overbid me, too.'

Paul did not lose his self-possession. Thanks to the fact that Yerba was not present, and that Don Cæsar, who had overheard the speech, moved forward with a suggestive and unpleasant smile, his agitation congealed into a coldly placid fury.

'And I suppose,' he returned, with perfect calmness, 'that, after the usual habit of this class of women, the necklace very soon found its way back, through the pawnbroker, to the jeweller again. It's a common fate.'

'Yes, of course,' said Judge Baker, cheerfully. 'You're quite right. That's undoubtedly the solution of it. But,' with a laugh, 'I had a narrow escape from saying something—eh?'

'A very narrow escape from an apparently gratuitous insult,' said Paul, gravely, but fixing his eyes, now more luminous than ever with anger, not on the speaker, but on the face of Don Cæsar, who was standing at his side. 'You were about to say'——

'Eh—oh—ah! this Kate Howard? So! I have heard of her—yees! And Miss Yerba—ah—she is of my country—I think. Yes—we shall claim her—of a truth—yes.'

'Your countrymen, I believe, are in the habit of making claims that are more often founded on profit than verity,' said Paul, with smileless and insulting deliberation. He knew perfectly what he was saying, and the result he expected. Only twenty-four hours before he had smiled at Pendleton's idea of averting scandal and discovery by fighting, yet he was

He was endeavouring to pick a quarrel with a man merely on suspicion

endeavouring to pick a quarrel with a man, merely on suspicion, for the same purpose, and he saw nothing strange in it. A vague idea too, that this would irrevocably confirm him in opposition to Yerba's illusions probably determined him.

But Don Cæsar, albeit smiling lividly, did not seem inclined to pick up the gauntlet, and Woods interfered hastily. 'Don Cæsar means that your ward has some idea herself that she is of Spanish origin—at least, Milly says so. But of course, as one of the oldest trustees, *you* know the facts.'

In another moment Paul would have committed himself. 'I think we'll leave Miss Yerba out of the question,' he said coldly. 'My remark was a general one, though, of course, I am responsible for any personal application of it.'

'Spoken like a politician, Hathaway,' said Judge Baker, with an effusive enthusiasm which he hoped would atone for the alarming results of his infelicitous speech. 'That's right, gentlemen! You can't get the facts from him before he is ready to give them. Keep your secret, Mr. Hathaway, the Court is with you.'

Nevertheless, as they passed out of the room to join the ladies, the Mayor lingered a little behind with Woods. It's easy to see the influence of that Pendleton on our young friend,' he said significantly. 'Somebody ought to tell him that it's played out down here—as Pendleton is. It's quite enough to ruin his career.'

Paul was too observant not to notice this, but it brought him no sense of remorse; and his youthful belief in himself and his power kept him from concern. He felt as if he had done something, if only to show Don Cæsar that the girl's weakness or ignorance could not be traded upon with impunity. But he was still undecided as to the course he should pursue. But he should determine that to-night. At present there seemed no chance of talking to her alone —she was unconcernedly conversing with Milly and Mrs. Woods, and already the visitors who had been invited to this hurried *levée* in his honour were arriving. In view of his late indiscretion, he nervously exerted his fullest powers, and in a very few minutes was surrounded by a breathless and admiring group of worshippers. A ludicrous resemblance to the scene in the Golden Gate Hotel passed through his mind; he involuntarily turned his eyes to seek Yerba in the half-fear, half-expectation of meeting her mischievous smile. Their glances met; to his surprise hers was smileless, and instantly withdrawn, but not until he had been thrilled by an unconscious prepossession in its luminous depths that he scarcely dared to dwell upon. What mattered now his passage with Don Cæsar or the plaudits of his friends? *She* was proud of him!

Yet, after that glance she was shy, preoccupying herself with Milly, or even listening sweetly to Judge Baker's somewhat practical and unromantic reminiscences of the deprivations and the hardships of Californian early days, as if to condone his past infelicity. She was pleasantly unaffected with Don Cæsar, although she managed to draw Doña Anna into the conversation; she was unconventional, Paul fancied, to all but himself. Once or twice, when he had artfully drawn her towards the open French windows that led to the moonlit garden and shadowed verandah, she had managed to link Milly's arm in her own, and he was confident that a suggestion to stroll with him in the open air would be followed by her invitation to Milly to accompany them. Disappointed and mortified as he was, he found some solace in her manner, which he still believed suggested the hope that she might be made accessible to his persuasions. Persuasions to what? He did not know.

The last guest had departed; he lingered on the verandah with a cigar, begging his host and hostess not to trouble themselves to keep him company. Milly and Yerba had retired to the former's boudoir, but, as they had not yet formally bade him good-night, there was a chance of their returning. He still stayed on in this hope for half an hour, and then, accepting Yerba's continued absence as a tacit refusal of his request, he turned abruptly away. But as he glanced around the garden before re-entering the house, he was struck by a singular circumstance—a white patch, like a forgotten shawl, which he had observed on the distant ceanothus hedge, and which had at first thrilled him with expectation, had certainly *changed its position*. Before, it seemed to be near the summer-house; now it was, undoubtedly, farther away. Could they, or *she* alone, have slipped from the house and be awaiting him there? With a muttered exclamation at his stupidity he stepped hastily from the verandah

He lingered on the verandah with a cigar

and walked towards it. But he had scarcely proceeded a dozen yards before it disappeared.

He reached the summer-house—it was empty he followed the line of hedge—no one was there. It could not have been her, or she would have waited—unless he were the victim of a practical joke. He turned impatiently back to the house, re-entered the drawing-room by the French window, and was crossing the half-lit apartment, when he heard a slight rustle in the shadow of the window. He looked around quickly, and saw that it was Yerba, in a white loose gown, for which she had already exchanged her black evening dress, leaning back composedly on the sofa, her hands clasped behind her shapely head.

'I am waiting for Milly,' she said, with a faint smile on her lips. He fancied, in the moonlight that streamed upon her, that her beautiful face was pale. 'She has gone to the other wing to see one of the servants who is ill. We thought you were on the verandah smoking and I should have company, until I saw you start off, and rush up and down the hedge like mad.'

Paul felt that he was losing his self-possession, and becoming nervous in her presence.

'I thought it was *you*,' he stammered.

'Me! Out in the garden at this hour, alone, and in the broad moonlight? What are you thinking of, Mr. Hathaway? Do you know anything of convent rules, or is that your idea of your ward's education?'

He fancied that, though she smiled faintly, her voice was as tremulous as his own.

'I want to speak with you,' he said, with awkward directness. 'I even thought of asking you to stroll with me in the garden.'

'Why not talk here?' she returned, changing her position, pointing to the other end of the sofa, and drawing the whole overflow of her skirt to one side. 'It is not so very late, and Milly will return in a few moments.'

Her face was in shadow now, but there was a glow-worm light in her beautiful eyes that seemed faintly to illuminate her whole face. He sank down on the sofa at her side, no longer the brilliant and ambitious politician, but, it seemed to him, as hopelessly a dreaming, inexperienced boy as when he had given her the name that now was all he could think of, and the only word that rose to his feverish lips.

'Yerba!'

'I like to hear you say it,' she said quickly, as if to gloss over his first omission of her formal prefix, and leaning a little forward, with her eyes on his. 'One would think you had created it. You almost make me regret to lose it.'

He stopped! He felt that the last sentence had saved him. 'It is of that I want to speak,' he broke out suddenly and almost rudely. 'Are you satisfied that it means nothing and can mean nothing, to you? Does it awaken no memory in your mind—recall nothing you care to know? Think! I beg you, I implore you to be frank with me!'

She looked at him with surprise.

'I have told you already that my present name must be some absurd blunder, or some intentional concealment. But why do you want to know *now*?' she continued, adding her faint smile to the emphasis.

'To help you!' he said eagerly. 'For that alone! To do all I can to assist you, if you really believe, and want to believe, that you have another. To ask you to confide in me;

to tell me all you have been told, all that you know, think you know, or *want* to know about your relationship to the Arguellos—or to anyone! And then to devote myself entirely to proving what you shall say is your desire. You see, I am frank with you, Yerba! I only ask you to be as frank with me: to let me know your doubts, that I may counsel you; your fears, that I may give you courage.'

'Is that all that you came here to tell me?' she asked quietly.

'No, Yerba,' he said eagerly, taking her unresisting but indifferent hand, 'not all; but all that I must say, all that I have the right to say, all that you, Yerba, would permit me to tell you *now*. But let me hope that the day is not far distant when I can tell you *all*, when you will understand that this silence has been the hardest sacrifice of the man who now speaks to you.'

'And yet not unworthy of a rising politician,' she added, quickly withdrawing her hand. 'I agree,' she went on, looking towards the door, yet without appearing to avoid his eager eyes, 'and when I have settled upon "a local habitation and a name" we shall renew this interesting conversation. Until then, as my fourth official guardian used to say—he was a lawyer, Mr. Hathaway, like yourself—when he was winding up his conjectures on the subject —all that has passed is to be considered "without prejudice"!'

'But, Yerba'—— began Paul, bitterly.

She slightly raised her hand as if to check him with a warning gesture. 'Yes, dear,' she said suddenly, lifting her musical voice, with a mischievous side-glance at Paul, as if to indicate her conception of the irony of a possible application, 'this way! Here we are waiting for you!' Her listening ear had detected Milly's step in the passage, and in another moment that cheerful young woman discreetly stopped on the threshold of the room, with every expression of apologetic indiscretion in her face.

'We have finished our talk, and Mr. Hathaway has been so concerned about my having no real name that he has been promising me everything, but his own, for a suitable one. Haven't you, Mr. Hathaway?' She rose slowly and, going over to Milly, put her arm around her waist and stood for one instant gazing at him between the curtains of the doorway. 'Good-night. My very proper chaperon is dreadfully shocked at this midnight interview, and is taking me away. Only think of it, Milly : he actually proposed to me to walk in the garden with him! Good-night, or, as my ancestors—don't forget, *my ancestors*—used to say: " *Buena noche—hasta mañana !* "' She lingered over the Spanish syllables with an imitation of Doña Anna's lisp, and with another smile, but more faint and more ghost-like than before, vanished with her companion.

At eight o'clock the next morning Paul was standing beside his portmanteau on the verandah.

'But this is a sudden resolution of yours, Hathaway,' said Mr. Woods. 'Can you not possibly wait for the next train? The girls will be down then, and you can breakfast comfortably.'

'I have much to do—more than I imagined —in San Francisco before I return,' said Paul, quickly. 'You must make my excuses to them and to your wife.'

'I hope you have had no more words with Don Cæsar'

'I hope,' said Woods, with an uneasy laugh, 'you have had no more words with Don Cæsar, or he with you?'

'No,' said Paul, with a reassuring smile, 'nothing more, I assure you.'

'For you know you're a devilish quick fellow, Hathaway,' continued Woods, 'quite as quick as your friend Pendleton. And, by the way, Baker is awfully cut up about that absurd speech of his, you know. Came to me last night and wondered if anybody could think it was intentional. I told him it was d—d stupid, that was all. I guess his wife had been at him. Ha! ha! You see, he remembers the old times, when everybody talked of these things, and that woman Howard was quite a character. I'm told she went off to the States years ago.'

'Possibly,' said Paul, carelessly. After a pause, as the carriage drove up to the door, he turned to his host. 'By the way, Woods, have you a ghost here?'

'The house is old enough for one. But, no. Why?'

'I'll swear I saw a figure moving yonder, in the shrubbery, late last evening; and when I came up to it, it most unaccountably disappeared.'

L

'One of Don Cæsar's servants, I dare say. There is one of them, an Indian, prowling about here, I've been told, at all hours. I'll put a stop to it. Well, you must go, then? Dreadfully sorry you couldn't stop longer! Good-bye!'

CHAPTER IV

IT was two months later that Mr. Tony Shear, of Marysville, but lately confidential clerk to the Hon. Paul Hathaway, entered his employer's chambers in Sacramento, and handed the latter a letter.

'I only got back from San Francisco this morning; but Mr. Slate said I was to give you that, and if it satisfied you, and was what you wanted, you would send it back to him.'

Paul took the envelope and opened it. It contained a printer's proof-slip, which he hurriedly glanced over. It read as follows:—

Those of our readers who are familiar with

the early history of San Francisco will be interested to know that an eccentric and irregular trusteeship, vested for the last eight

A printer's proof slip, which he hurriedly glanced over

years in the Mayor of San Francisco and two of our oldest citizens, was terminated yesterday by the majority of a beautiful and accomplished young lady, a pupil of the Convent of Santa Clara. Very few, except the original trustees, were cognisant of the fact that the administration of the trustees has been a recognised function of the successive Mayors of San Francisco during this period; and the mystery surrounding it has been only lately divulged. It offers a touching and romantic instance of a survival of the old patriarchal duties of the former *Alcaldes* and the simplicity of pioneer days. It seems that, in the unsettled conditions of the Mexican land-titles that followed the American occupation, the consumptive widow of a scion of one of the oldest Californian families entrusted her property and the custody of her infant daughter virtually to the City of San Francisco, as represented by the trustees specified, until the girl should become of age. Within a year, the invalid mother died. With what loyalty, sagacity, and prudence these gentlemen fulfilled their trust may be gathered from the fact that the property left in their charge has not only been secured and protected, but increased a hundredfold in value; and that the young lady who yesterday attained her majority is not only one of the richest landed heiresses on the Pacific Slope, but one of the most accomplished and thoroughly educated of her sex. It is now no secret that this favoured child of Chrysopolis is the Doña Maria Concepcion de Arguello de la Yerba Buena, so called from her ancestral property on the island, now owned by the Federal Government. But it is an affecting and poetic tribute to the parent of her adoption that she has preferred to pass under the old, quaintly typical name of the city, and has been known to her friends simply as 'Miss Yerba Buena.' It is a no less pleasant and suggestive circumstance that our 'youngest Senator,' the Honourable Paul Hathaway, formerly private secretary to Mayor Hammersley, is one of the original unofficial trustees; while the chivalry of the older days is perpetuated in the person of Colonel Harry Pendleton, the remaining trustee.

As soon as he had finished, Paul took a pencil and crossed out the last six lines; but instead of laying the proof aside, or returning it to the waiting secretary, he remained with it in his hand, his silent, set face turned towards the window. Whether the merely human secretary was tired of waiting, or the devoted partisan saw something on his young chief's face that disturbed him, he turned to Paul with that exaggerated respect which his functions as secretary had grafted upon his affection for his old associate, and said—

'I hope nothing's wrong, Sir. Not another of those scurrilous attacks on you for putting that Bill through to relieve Colonel Pendleton? Yet it was a risky thing for you, Sir.'

Paul started, recovered himself as if from some remote abstraction, and, with a smile, said: 'No—nothing. Quite the reverse. Write to Mr. Slate, thank him, and say that it will do very well—with the exception of the lines I have marked out. Then bring me the letter, and I will add this enclosure. Did you call on Colonel Pendleton?'

'Yes, Sir. He was at Santa Clara, and had not yet returned—at least, that's what that dandy nigger of his told me. The airs and graces that that creature puts on since the Colonel's affairs have been straightened out is a little too much for a white man to stand.

Why, Sir! d——d if he didn't want to patronise *you*, and allowed to me that "de Kernel" had a "fah ideah" of you, "and thought you a promisin' young man." The fact is, Sir, the Party is making a big mistake trying to give votes to that kind of cattle—it would only be giving two votes to the other side, for, slave or free, they're the chattels of their old masters. And as to the masters' gratitude for what you've done affecting a single vote of their Party—you're mistaken.'

'Colonel Pendleton belongs to no Party,' said Paul, curtly; 'but if his old constituents ever try to get into power again, they've lost their only independent martyr.'

He presently became abstracted again, and Shear produced from his overcoat pocket a series of official-looking documents.

'I've brought the reports, Sir.'

'Eh?' said Paul, absently.

The secretary stared. 'The reports of the San Francisco Chief of Police that you asked me to get.' His employer was certainly very forgetful to-day.

'Oh, yes; thank you. You can lay them

on my desk. I'll look them over in Committee. You can go now, and if anyone calls to see me say I am busy.'

The secretary disappeared in the adjoining room, and Paul leaned back in his chair, thinking. He had, at last, effected the work he had resolved upon when he left Rosario two months ago; the article he had just read, and which would appear as an editorial in the San Francisco paper the day after to-morrow, was the culmination of quietly persistent labour, inquiry, and deduction, and would be accepted, hereafter, as authentic history, which, if not thoroughly established, at least could not be gainsaid. Immediately on arriving at San Francisco, he had hastened to Pendleton's bedside, and laid the facts and his plan before him. To his mingled astonishment and chagrin, the Colonel had objected vehemently to this 'saddling of anybody's offspring on a gentleman who couldn't defend himself,' and even Paul's explanation that the putative father was a myth scarcely appeased him. But Paul's timely demonstration, by relating the scene he had witnessed of Judge Baker's infelicitous memory, that the secret was likely to be revealed at any moment, and that if the girl continued to cling to her theory, as he feared she would, even to the parting with her fortune, they would be forced to accept it, or be placed in the hideous position of publishing her disgrace, at last convinced him. On the other hand, there was less danger of her *positive* imposition being discovered than of the *vague and impositive* truth. The real danger lay in the present uncertainty and mystery, which courted surmise and invited discovery. Paul, himself, was willing to take all the responsibility, and at last extracted from the Colonel a promise of passive assent. The only revelation he feared was from the interference of the mother, but Pendleton was strong in the belief that she had not only utterly abandoned the girl to the care of her guardians, but that she would never rescind her resolution to disclaim her relationship; that she had gone into self-exile for that purpose; and that if she *had* changed her mind he would be the first to know of it. On this they had parted. Meantime, Paul had not forgotten another resolution he had formed on his first visit to the Colonel, and had actually succeeded in getting Legislative relief for the Golden Gate Bank, and restoring to the Colonel some of his private property that had been in the hands of a Receiver.

This had been the background of Paul's meditation, which only threw into stronger relief the face and figure that moved before him as persistently as it had once before in the twilight of his room at Rosario. There were times when her moonlit face, with its faint strange smile, stood out before him as it had stood out of the shadows of the half-darkened drawing-room that night; as he had seen it—he believed for the last time—framed for an instant in the parted curtains of the doorway, when she bade him 'Good-night.' For he had never visited her since, and, on the attainment of her majority, had delegated his passing functions to Pendleton, whom he had induced to accompany the Mayor to Santa Clara for the final and formal ceremony. For the present she need not know how much she had been indebted to him for the accomplishment of her wishes.

With a sigh he at last recalled himself to his

duty, and, drawing the pile of reports which Shear had handed him, he began to examine them. These, again, bore reference to his silent, unobtrusive inquiries. In his function as Chairman of Committee he had taken advantage of a kind of advanced moral legislation then in vogue, and particularly in reference to a certain social reform, to examine statistics, authorities, and witnesses, and in this indirect but exhaustive manner had satisfied himself that the woman ' Kate Howard,' alias ' Beverley,' alias ' Durfree,' had long passed beyond the ken of local police supervision, and that in the record there was no trace or indication of her child. He was going over those infelix records of early transgressions with the eye of trained experience, making notes from time no time for his official use, and yet always watchful of his secret quest, when suddenly he stopped with a quickened pulse. In the record of an affray at a gambling-house, one of the parties had sought refuge in the room of ' Kate Howard,' who was represented before the magistrate by *her protector*, *Juan de Arguello*. The date given was contemporary with the beginning of the Trust, but that proved nothing. But the name—had it any significance, or was it a grim coincidence, that spoke even more terribly and hopelessly of the woman's promiscuous frailty? He again attacked the entire report, but there was no other record of her name. Even that would have passed any eye less eager and watchful than his own.

He laid the reports aside, and took up the proof-slip again. Was there any man living but himself and Pendleton who would connect these two statements? That her relations with this Arguello were brief and not generally known was evident from Pendleton's ignorance of the fact. But he must see him again, and at once. Perhaps he might have acquired some information from Yerba; the young girl might have given to his age that confidence she had withheld from the younger man; indeed, he remembered with a flush it was partly in that hope that he had induced the Colonel to go to Santa Clara. He put the proof-slip in his pocket and stepped to the door of the next room.

'You need not write that letter to Slate'

Tony. I will see him myself. I am going to San Francisco to-night.'

'And do you want anything copied from the reports, Sir?'

Paul quickly swept them from the table into his drawer, and locked it. 'Not now, thank you. I'll finish my notes later.'

The next morning Paul was in San Francisco, and had again crossed the portals of the Golden Gate Hotel. He had been already told that the doom of that palatial edifice was sealed by the laying of the corner-stone of a new erection in the next square that should utterly eclipse it; he even fancied that it had already lost its freshness, and its meretricious glitter had been tarnished. But when he had ordered his breakfast he made his way to the public parlour, happily deserted at that early hour. It was here that he had first seen her. She was standing there, by that mirror, when their eyes first met in a sudden instinctive sympathy. She herself had remembered and confessed it. He recalled the pleased yet conscious girlish superiority with which she had received the adulation of her friends; his memory of her was broad enough now even to identify Milly, as it repeopled the vacant and silent room.

An hour later he was making his way to Colonel Pendleton's lodgings, and half-expecting to find the St. Charles' Hotel itself transformed by the eager spirit of improvement. But it was still there in all its barbaric and provincial incongruity. Public opinion had evidently recognised that nothing save the absolute razing of its warped and flimsy walls could effect a change, and waited for it to collapse suddenly like the house of cards it resembled. Paul wondered for a moment if it were not ominous of its lodgers' hopeless inability to accept changed conditions, and it was with a feeling of doubt that he even now ascended the creaking staircase. But it was instantly dissipated on the threshold of the Colonel's sitting-room by the appearance of George and his reception of his master's guest.

The grizzled negro was arrayed in a surprisingly new suit of blue cloth with a portentous white waistcoat and an enormous crumpled white cravat, that gave him the appearance of suffering from a glandular swelling. His manner had, it seemed to Paul, advanced in exaggeration, with his clothes. Dusting a chair and offering it to the visitor, he remained gracefully posed with his hand on the back of another.

'Yo finds us heah yet, Marse Hathaway,' he began, elegantly toying with an enormous silver watch-chain, 'fo' de Kernel he don' bin find contagious apartments dat at all approximate, and he don' build, for his mind's not dat settled dat he ain't goin' to trabbel. De place is low down, Sah, and de fo'ks is low down, and dah's a heap o' white trash dat has congested under de roof ob de hotel since we came. But we uses it temper'ly, Sah, fo' de present, and in a dissolutory fashion.'

It struck Paul that the contiguity of a certain barber's shop and its dangerous reminiscences had something to do with George's lofty depreciation of his surroundings, and he could not help saying—

'Then you don't find it necessary to have it convenient to the barber's shop any more? I am glad of that, George.'

The shot told. The unfortunate George, after an endeavour to collect himself by altering s pose two or three times in rapid succession, ially collapsed, and with an air of mingled in and dignity, but without losing his ceremoous politeness or unique vocabulary, said—

'Yo got me dah, Sah! Yo got me dah! e infirmities o' human natcheh, Sah, is de ommon p'operty ob man, and a gemplum like o'self, Sah, a legislato' and a pow'ful speakah, de lass one to hol' it agin de individal pusson. confess, Sah, de circumstances was propisious, de fees fahly good, and de risks inferior. e gemplum who kept de shop was an artess sself, an' had been niggah to Kernel Henrson of Tennessee, and de gemplum I relieved as a Mr. Johnson. But de Kernel, he ouldn't see it in that light, Sah, and if you n' mind, Sah'—

'I haven't the slightest idea of telling the olonel or anybody, George,' said Paul smiling; nd I am glad to find on your own account at you are able to put aside any work beyond ur duty here.'

'Thank you, Sah. If yo'll let me introduce to de refreshment, yo'll find it all right now. e Glencoe is dah. De Kernel will be here

M

soon, but he would be pow'ful mo'tified, Sah, if yo didn't hab something afo' he come.' He opened a well-filled sideboard as he spoke. It

'Yo got me dah, Sah! Yo got me dah!'

was the first evidence Paul had seen of the Colonel's restored fortunes. He would willingly have contented himself with this mere outward

manifestation, but in his desire to soothe the
ruffled dignity of the old man he consented to

George at once became communicative

partake of a small glass of spirits. George at
once became radiant and communicative. 'De
Kernel bin gone to Santa Clara to see de young

lady dat's finished her edercation dah—de Kernel's only ward, Sah. She's one o' dose million-heiresses and highly connected, Sah, wid de old Mexican Gobbermen, I understand. And I reckon dey's bin big goin's on doun dar, foh de Mayer kem hisself fo' de Kernel. Looks like dey might bin a proceshon, Sah. Yo don' know if de young lady bin hab a title, Sah? I won't be shuah, his Honah de Mayer or de Kernel didn't say something about a "Donna."'

'Very likely,' said Paul, turning away with a faint smile. So it was already in the air! Setting aside the old negro's characteristic exaggeration, there had already been some conversation between the Colonel and the Mayor, which George had vaguely overheard. He might be too late, the alternative might be no longer in his hands. But his discomposure was heightened a moment later by the actual apparition of the returning Pendleton.

He was dressed in a tightly-buttoned blue frock-coat, which fairly accented his tall, thin, military figure, although the top lappel was thrown far enough back to show a fine ruffled cambric shirt and checked gingham necktie, and was itself adorned with a white rosebud

He was dressed in a tightly-buttoned blue frock-coat

in the button-hole. Fawn-coloured trousers strapped over narrow patent-leather boots, and a tall white hat, whose broad mourning-band was a perpetual memory of his mother, who had died in his boyhood, completed his festal transformation. Yet his erect carriage, high aquiline nose, and long grey drooping moustache lent a distinguishing grace to this survival of a bygone fashion, and overrode any irreverent comment. Even his slight limp seemed to give a peculiar character to his massive gold-headed stick, and made it a part of his formal elegance.

Handing George his stick and a military cape he carried easily over his left arm, he greeted Paul warmly, yet with a return of his old dominant manner.

'Glad to see you, Hathaway, and glad to see the boy has served you better than the last time. If I had known you were coming, I would have tried to get back in time to have breakfast with you. But your friends at 'Rosario'—I think they call it; in my time it was owned by Colonel Briones, and *he* called it 'The Devil's Little Cañon'—detained me with some d—d civilities. Let's see—his name is Woods, isn't it? Used to sell rum to runaway sailors on Long Wharf, and take stores in exchange? Or was it Baker?—Judge Baker? I forget which. Well, Sir, they wished to be remembered.'

It struck Paul, perhaps unreasonably, that the Colonel's indifference and digression were both a little assumed, and he asked abruptly—

'And you fulfilled your mission?'

'I made the formal transfer, with the Mayor, of the property to Miss Arguello.'

'To Miss Arguello?'

'To the Doña Maria Concepcion de Arguello de la Yerba Buena—to speak precisely,' said the Colonel slowly. 'George, you can take that hat to that blank hatter—what's his blanked name?—I read it only yesterday in a list of the prominent citizens here—and tell him, with my compliments, that I want a *gentleman's* mourning band around my hat, and not a child's shoelace. It may be *his* idea of the value of his own parents—if he ever had any—but I don't care for him to appraise mine. Go!'

As the door closed upon George, Paul turned to the Colonel—

'Then am I to understand that you have agreed to her story?'

The Colonel rose, picked up the decanter, poured out a glass of whisky, and, holding it in his hand, said—

The Colonel poured out a glass of whisky

'My dear Hathaway, let us understand each

other. As a gentleman, I have made a point through life never to question the age, name, or family of any lady of my acquaintance. Miss Yerba Buena came of age yesterday, and, as she is no longer my ward, she is certainly entitled to the consideration I have just mentioned. If she, therefore, chooses to tack to her name the whole Spanish directory, I don't see why I shouldn't accept it.'

Characteristic as this speech appeared to be of the Colonel's ordinary manner, it struck Paul as being only an imitation of his usual frank independence, and made him uneasily conscious of some vague desertion on Pendleton's part. He fixed his bright eyes on his host, who was ostentatiously sipping his liquor, and said—

'Am I to understand that you have heard nothing more from Miss Yerba, either for or against her story? That you still do not know whether she has deceived herself, has been deceived by others, or is deceiving us?'

'After what I have just told you, Mr. Hathaway,' said the Colonel, with an increased exaggeration of manner which Paul thought must be apparent even to himself, 'I should have but one way of dealing with questions of that kind from anybody but yourself.'

This culminating extravagance—taken in connection with Pendleton's passing doubts—actually forced a laugh from Paul in spite of his bitterness.

Colonel Pendleton's face flushed quickly. Like most positive one-idea'd men, he was restricted from any possible humorous combination, and only felt a mysterious sense of being detected in some weakness. He put down his glass.

'Mr. Hathaway,' he began, with a slight vibration in his usual dominant accents, 'you have lately put me under a sense of personal obligation for a favour which I felt I could accept without derogation from a younger man, because it seemed to be one not only of youthful generosity but of justice, and was not unworthy the exalted ambition of a young man like yourself or the simple deserts of an old man such as I am. I accepted it, Sir, the more readily, because it was entirely unsolicited by me, and seemed to be the spontaneous offering of your own heart. If I have presumed upon it to express myself freely on other matters in a way that only excites your ridicule, I can but offer you an apology, Sir. If I have accepted a favour I can neither renounce nor return, I must take the consequences to myself, and even beg *you*, Sir, to put up with them.'

Remorseful as Paul felt, there was a singular resemblance between the previous reproachful pose of George and this present attitude of his master, as if the mere propinquity of personal sacrifice had made them alike, that struck him with a mingled pathos and ludicrousness. But he said warmly: 'It is I who must apologise, my dear Colonel. I am not laughing at your conclusions, but at this singular coincidence with a discovery I have made.'

'As how, Sir?'

'I find in the report of the Chief of the Police for the year 1850 that Kate Howard was under the protection of a man named Arguello.'

The Colonel's exaggeration instantly left him. He stared blankly at Paul. 'And you call this a laughing matter, Sir?' he said sternly, but in his more natural manner.

'Perhaps not, but I don't think, if you will allow me to say so, my dear Colonel, that *you* have been treating the whole affair very seriously. I left you two months ago utterly opposed to views which you are now treating as of no importance. And yet you wish me to believe that nothing has happened, and that you have no further information than you had then. That this is so, and that you are really no nearer the *facts*, I am willing to believe from your ignorance of what I have just told you, and your concern at it. But that you have not been influenced in your *judgment* of what you do know, I cannot believe?' He drew nearer Pendleton, and laid his hand upon his arm. 'I beg you to be frank with me, for the sake of the person whose interests I see you have at heart. In what way will the discovery I have just made affect them? You are not so far prejudiced as to be blind to the fact that it may be dangerous because it seems corroborative.'

Pendleton coughed, rose, took his stick, and limped up and down the room, finally dropping into an arm-chair by the window, with his cane between his knees, and the drooping grey silken threads of his long moustache curled nervously between his fingers.

'Mr. Hathaway, I *will* be frank with you. I know nothing of this blank affair—blank it all!—but what I've told you. Your discovery may be a coincidence, nothing more. But I *have* been influenced, Sir—influenced by one of the most perfect, goddess-like—yes, Sir; one of the most simple girlish creatures that God ever sent upon earth. A woman that I should be proud to claim as my daughter, a woman that would always be the superior of any man who dare aspire to be her husband! A young lady as peerless in her beauty as she is in her accomplishments, and whose equal don't walk this planet! I know, Sir, *you* don't follow me; I know, Mr. Hathaway, your Puritan prejudices; your Church proclivities; your worldly sense of propriety; and, above all, Sir, the blanked hypocritical, Pharisaic doctrines of your party —I mean no offence to *you*, Sir, personally— blind you to that girl's perfections. She, poor child, herself has seen it and felt it; but never, in her blameless innocence and purity, suspecting the cause. "There is," she said to me last night, confidentially, "something strangely antagonistic and repellent in our natures, some undefined and nameless barrier between our ever understanding each other." You comprehend, Mr. Hathaway, she does full justice to your intentions and your unquestioned abilities. "I am not blind," she said, "to Mr. Hathaway's gifts, and it is very possible the fault lies with me." Her very words, Sir.'

'Then you believe she is perfectly ignorant of her real mother?' asked Paul, with a steady voice, but a whitening face.

'As an unborn child,' said the Colonel, emphatically. 'The snow on the Sierras is not more spotlessly pure of any trace or contamination of the mud of the mining ditches, than she of her mother and her past. The knowledge of it, the mere breath of suspicion of it, in her presence would be a profanation, Sir! Look at her eye—open as the sky and as clear; look at her face and figure—as clean, Sir, as a Blue-Grass thoroughbred! Look at the way she carries herself, whether in those white frillings of her simple school-gown, or that black evening dress that makes her look like a Princess! And, blank me, if she isn't one! There's no poor stock there—no white trash—no mixed blood, Sir. Blank it all, Sir, if it comes to *that*—the Arguellos—if there's a hound of them living—might go down on their knees to have their name borne by such a creature! By the Eternal, Sir, if one of them dared to cross her path with a word that wasn't abject—yes, Sir, *abject*, I'd wipe his dust off the earth and send it back to his ancestors before he knew where he was, or my name isn't Harry Pendleton!'

Hopeless and inconsistent as all this was, it was a wonderful sight to see the Colonel, his dark, stern face illuminated with a zealot's enthusiasm, his eyes on fire, the ends of his grey moustache curling around his set jaw, his head thrown back, his legs astride, and his gold-headed stick held in the hollow of his elbow, like a lance at rest! Paul saw it, and knew that this Quixotic transformation was part of *her* triumph, and yet had a miserable consciousness that the charms of this Dulcinea del Toboso had scarcely been exaggerated. He turned his eyes away, and said quietly—

'Then you don't think this coincidence will

ever awaken any suspicion in regard to her real mother?'

'Not in the least, Sir—not in the least,' said the Colonel, yet, perhaps, with more doggedness than conviction of accent. 'Nobody but yourself would ever notice that police report, and the connection of that woman's name with his was not notorious, or I should have known it.'

'And you believe,' continued Paul, hopelessly, 'that Miss Yerba's selection of the name was purely accidental?'

'Purely—a schoolgirl's fancy. Fancy, did I say? No, Sir; by Jove, an inspiration!'

'And,' continued Paul, almost mechanically, 'you do not think it may be some insidious suggestion of an enemy who knew of this transient relation that no one suspected?'

To his final amazement Pendleton's brow cleared! 'An enemy? Gad! you may be right. I'll look into it; and, if that is the case, which I scarcely dare hope for, Mr. Hathaway, you can safely leave him to *me*.'

He looked so supremely confident in his fatuous heroism that Paul could say no more.

He rose and, with a faint smile upon his pale face, held out his hand. 'I think that is all I have to say. When you see Miss Yerba again —as you will, no doubt—you may tell her that I am conscious of no misunderstanding on my part, except, perhaps, as to the best way I could serve her, and that, but for what she has told *you*, I should certainly have carried away no remembrance of any misunderstanding of *hers*.'

'Certainly,' said the Colonel, with cheerful philosophy, 'I will carry your message with pleasure. You understand how it is, Mr. Hathaway. There is no accounting for these instincts —we can only accept them as they are. But I believe that your intentions, Sir, were strictly according to what you conceived to be your duty. You won't take something before you go? Well, then—good-bye.'

Two weeks later Paul found among his morning letters an envelope addressed in Colonel Pendleton's boyish scrawling hand. He opened it with an eagerness that no studied self-control nor rigid preoccupation of his duties had yet been able to subdue, and glanced hurriedly at its contents :—

Dear Sir,—As I am on the point of sailing for Europe to-morrow to escort Miss Arguello and Miss Woods on an extended visit to England and the Continent, I am desirous of informing you that I have thus far been unable to find any foundation for the suggestions thrown out by you in our last interview. Miss Arguello's Spanish acquaintances have been very select, and limited to a few school friends and Don Cæsar and Doña Anna Briones, tried friends, who are also fellow-passengers with us to Europe. Miss Arguello suggests that some political difference between you and Don Cæsar, which occurred during your visit to Rosario three months ago, may have, perhaps, given rise to your supposition. She joins me in best wishes for your public career, which even in the distractions of foreign travel and the obligations of her position she will follow from time to time with the greatest interest.—Very respectfully yours,

HARRY PENDLETON.

CHAPTER V

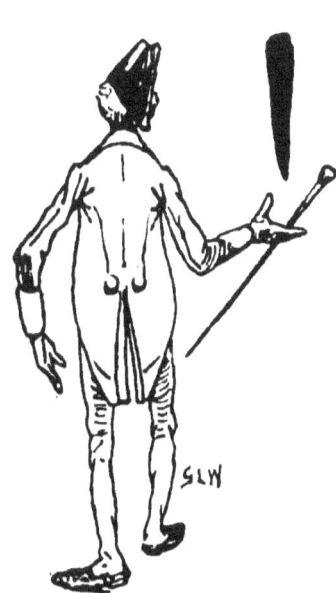

IT was on an August day of 1863 that Paul Hathaway resigned himself and his luggage to the care of the gold-laced, ostensible porter of the Strudle Bad Hof, not without some uncertainty, in a land of uniforms, whether he would eventually be conducted to the barracks, the police office, or the Conservatoire. He was relieved when the omnibus drove into the courtyard of the Bad Hof, and the gold-chained chamberlain, flanked by two green tubs of oleanders, received him with a gravity calculated to check any preconceived idea he might have that travelling was a trifling affair, or that an arrival at the Bad Hof was not of serious moment. His letters had not yet arrived, for he had, in a fit of restlessness, shortened his route, and he strolled listlessly into the reading-room. Two or three English guests were evidently occupied in eminently respectable reading and writing; two were sitting by the window engaged in subdued but profitable conversation; and two Americans from Boston were contentedly imitating them on the other side of the room. A decent restraint, as of people who were not for a moment to be led into any foreign idea of social gaiety at a watering-place, was visible everywhere. A spectacled Prussian officer in full uniform passed along the hall, halted for a moment at the door-way as if contemplating an armed invasion, thought better of it, and took his uniform away into the sunlight of the open square, where it was joined by other uniforms, and became by contrast a miracle of unbraced levity. Paul stood the Polar silence for a few moments, until one of the readers arose and, taking his book,—a Murray—in his hand, walked slowly across the room to a companion, mutely pointed to a passage in the book, remained silent until the other had dumbly perused it, and then walked back

Halted a moment at the doorway

again to his seat, having achieved the incident without a word. At which Paul, convinced of his own incongruity, softly withdrew with his hat in his hand, and his eyes fixed devotionally upon it.

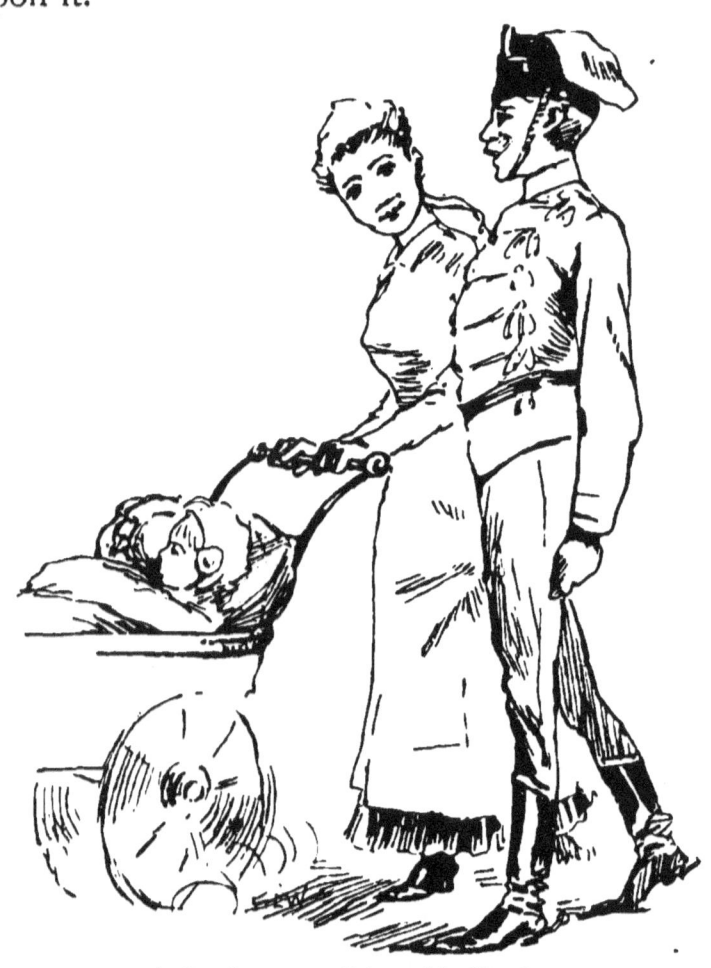

A Cavalryman walking with Clärchen

It was good after that to get into the slanting sunlight and chequered linden shadows of the

Allee; to see even a tightly jacketed cavalryman naturally walking with Clärchen and her two round-faced and drab-haired young charges; to watch the returning invalid procession, very real and very human, each individual intensely involved in the atmosphere of his own symptoms; and very good after that to turn into the Thiergarten, where the animals were, however, chiefly of his own species, and shamelessly and openly amusing themselves. It was pleasant to contrast it with his first visit to the place three months before, and correct his crude impressions. And it was still more pleasant suddenly to recognise, under the round flat cap of a general officer, a former traveller who was fond of talking with him about America with an intelligence and understanding of it that Paul had often missed among his own travelled countrymen. It was pleasant to hear his unaffected and simple greeting, to renew their old acquaintance, and to saunter back to the hotel together through the long twilight.

They were only a few squares from the hotel, when Paul's attention was attracted by the curiosity and delight of two or three children before him, who seemed to be following a quaint-looking figure that was evidently not un-

His unaffected and simple greeting

familiar to them. It appeared to be a servant in a striking livery of green with yellow facings and crested silver buttons, but still more remarkable for the indescribable mingling of jaunty ease and conscious dignity with which he carried off his finery. There was something so singular and yet so vaguely reminiscent in his peculiar walk and the exaggerated swing of his light bamboo cane that Paul could not only understand the childish wonder of the passers-by, who turned to look after him, but was stirred with a deeper curiosity. He quickened his pace, but was unable to distinguish anything of the face or features of the stranger, except that his hair under his cocked hat appeared to be tightly curled and powdered. Paul's companion, who was amused at what seemed to be the American's national curiosity, had seen the figure before. 'A servant in the suite of some Eastern *Altesse* visiting the baths. You will see stranger things, my friend, in the Strudle Bad. *Par exemple*, your own countrymen, too; the one who has enriched himself by that pork of Chicago, or that soap, or this candle, in a carriage with the crest of the title he has bought in Italy, with his dollars, and his beautiful daughters, who are seeking more titles with possible matrimonial contingencies.'

After an early dinner, Paul found his way to the little theatre. He had already been struck by a highly coloured poster near the *Bahnhof*, purporting that a distinguished German company would give a representation of 'Uncle Tom's Cabin,' and certain peculiarities in the pictorial advertisement of the tableaux gave promise of some entertainment. He found the theatre fairly full: there was the usual contingent of *abonnirte* officers, a fair sprinkling of English and German travellers, but apparently none of his own countrymen. He had no time to examine the house more closely, for the play, commencing with simple punctuality, not only far exceeded the promise of the posters, but of any previous performance of the play he had witnessed. Transported at once to a gorgeous tropical region—the Slave States of America—resplendent with the fruits and palms of Mauritius, and peopled exclusively with Paul and Virginia's companions in striped cotton, Hathaway managed to keep a composed face, until the arrival of the good Southern planter

St. Clair as one of the earlier portraits of Goethe, in top boots, light kerseymere breeches, redingote and loose Byron collar, compelled him to shrink into the upper corner of the box with his handkerchief to his face. Luckily, the action passed as the natural effect upon a highly sympathetic nature of religious interviews between a round-faced flaxen-haired 'Kleine Eva' and 'Onkeel Tome,' occasionally assisted by a Dissenting clergyman in Geneva bands; of excessive brutality with a cattle whip by a Zamiel-like Legree; of the sufferings of a runaway negro *Zimmermädchen* with a child three shades lighter than herself; and of a painted canvas 'man-hunt,' where apparently four well-known German composers on horseback, with flowing hair, top boots, and a *cor de chasse*, were pursuing, with the aid of a pack of foxhounds, 'the much too deeply abused and yet spiritually elevated Onkeel Tome.' Paul did not wait for the final apotheosis of 'der Kleine Eva,' but, in the silence of a hushed audience, made his way into the corridor and down the staircase. He was passing an open door marked 'Direction,' when his attention was sharply attracted by a small gathering around it, and the sounds of indignant declamation. It was the voice of a countryman—more than that, it was a familiar voice, that he had not heard for three years—the voice of Colonel Harry Pendleton!

'Tell him,' said Pendleton, in scathing tones, to some invisible interpreter—'tell him, Sir, that a more infamous caricature of the blankest caricature that ever maligned a free people, Sir, I never before had the honour of witnessing. Tell him that *I*, Sir—I, Harry Pendleton, of Kentucky, a Southerner, Sir—an old slaveholder, Sir, declare it to be a tissue of falsehoods unworthy the credence of a Christian civilisation like this—unworthy the attention of the distinguished ladies and gentlemen that are gathered here to-night. Tell him, Sir, he has been imposed upon. Tell him I am responsible—give him my card and address—personally responsible for what I say. If he wants proofs—blank it all!—tell him you yourself have been a slave—*my* slave, Sir! Take off your hat, Sir! Ask him to look at you—ask him if he thinks you ever looked or could look like that lop-eared, psalm-singing, white-headed hypocrite on the stage! Ask him, Sir, if he thinks that blank ringmaster they call St. Clair looks like *Me*!'

At this astounding exordium Paul eagerly pressed forward and entered the bureau. There certainly was Colonel Pendleton, in spotless evening dress; erect, flashing, and indignant; his aquiline nose lifted like a hawk's beak over his quarry, his iron-grey moustache, now white and waxed, parted like a swallow's tail over his handsome mouth, and between him and the astounded 'Direction' stood the apparition of the *Allee*—George! There was no mistaking him now. What Paul had thought was a curled wig or powder was the old negro's own white knotted wool and the astounding livery he wore was carried off as no one but George could carry it.

But he was still more amazed when the old servant, in a German as exaggerated, as incoherent, but still as fluent and persuasive as his own native speech, began an extravagant but perfectly dignified and diplomatic translation of his master's protests. Where and when, and by what instinct, he had assimilated and made his own the grotesque inversions and ponderous sentimentalities of Teutonic phrasing, Paul could not guess; but it was with breathless wonder that he presently became aware that, so perfect and convincing was the old man's style and deportment, not only the simple officials but even the bystanders were profoundly impressed by this farrago of absurdity. A happy word here and there, the full title and rank given, even with a slight exaggeration, to each individual, brought a deep and guttural 'So!' from lips that would have found it difficult to repeat a line of his ceremonious idiocy.

In their preoccupation neither the Colonel nor George had perceived Paul's entrance, but, as the old servant turned with magnificent courtesy towards the bystanders, his eyes fell upon Paul. A flash of surprise, triumph, and satisfaction lit up his rolling eyes. Paul instantly knew that he not only recognised him, but that he had already heard of and thoroughly appreciated a certain distinguished position that Paul had lately held, and was quick to apply it.

Intensifying for a moment the grandiloquence of his manner, he called upon his master's most distinguished and happily arrived old friend, the Lord Lieutenant Governor of the Golden Californias, to corroborate his statement. Colonel Pendleton started, and grasped Paul's hand warmly. Paul turned to the already half-mollified Director with the diplomatic suggestion that the vivid and realistic acting of the admirable company which he himself had witnessed had perhaps unduly excited his old friend, even as it had undoubtedly thrown into greater relief the usual exaggerations of dramatic representation, and the incident terminated with a profusion of apologies, and the most cordial expressions of international good feeling on both sides.

Yet, as they turned away from the theatre together, Paul could not help noticing that, although the Colonel's first greeting had been spontaneous and unaffected, it was succeeded by an uneasy reserve. Paul made no attempt to break it, and confined himself to a few general inquiries, ending by inviting the Colonel to sup with him at the hotel. Pendleton hesitated.

'At any other time, Mr. Hathaway, I should have insisted upon you, as the stranger, supping

They turned away together

with me; but since the absence of—of—the rest of my party—I have given up my suite of rooms at the Bad Hof, and have taken smaller lodgings for myself and the boy at the Schwartze Adler. Miss Woods and Miss Arguello have accepted an invitation to spend a few days at the villa of the Baron and Baroness von Schilprecht—an hour or two from here.' He lingered over the title with an odd mingling of impressiveness and inquiry, and glanced at Paul. But Hathaway exhibiting neither emotion nor surprise at the mention of Yerba's name or the title of her host, he continued, ' Miss Arguello, I suppose you know, is immensely admired ; she has been, Sir, the acknowledged belle of Strudle Bad.'

' I can readily believe it,' said Paul simply.

' And has taken the position—the position, Sir, to which she is entitled.'

Without appearing to notice the slight challenge in Pendleton's tone, Paul returned, ' I am glad to hear it. The more particularly as, I believe, the Germans are great sticklers for position and pedigree.'

' You are right, Sir—quite right : they are,'

o

said the Colonel, proudly—'although'—with a certain premeditated deliberation—' I have been credibly informed that the King can, in certain cases, if he chooses, supply—yes, Sir—*supply* a favoured person with ancestors—yes, Sir, with *ancestors*!'

Paul cast a quick glance at his companion.

'Yes, Sir—that is, we will say, in the case of a lady of inferior rank—or even birth, the King of these parts can, on her marriage with a nobleman—blank it all!—ennoble her father and mother, and their fathers and mothers, though they've been dead, or as good as dead, for years.'

'I am afraid that's a slight exaggeration of the rare custom of granting "noble lands," or estates that carry hereditary titles with them,' said Paul, more emphatically, perhaps, than the occasion demanded.

'Fact, Sir—George there knows it all,' said Pendleton. 'He gets it from the other servants. I don't speak the language, Sir, but *he* does. Picked it up in a year.'

'I must compliment him on his fluency, certainly,' said Paul, looking at George.

The old servant smiled, yet not without a certain condescension. 'Yes, Sah; I don' say to a scholar like yo'self, Sah, dat I'se got de grandmatical presichion; but as fah, Sah—as fah as de *idiotisms* ob de language goes, Sah— it's gen'lly allowed I'm dar! As to what Marse Harry says ob de ignobling ob predecessors, I've had it, Sah, from de best autority, Sah— de furst, I may say, Sah—de real *primâ facie* men—de gemplum ob his Serene Highness, in de korse ob ordinary conversashun, Sah.'

'That'll do, George,' said Pendleton, with paternal brusqueness. 'Run on ahead and tell that blank chamberlain that Mr. Hathaway is one of my friends—and have supper accordingly.' As the negro hastened away he turned to Paul: 'What he says is true: he's the most popular man or boy in all Strudle Bad—a devilish s'ght more than his master—and goes anywhere where *I* can't go. Princes and Princesses stop and talk to him in the street; the Grand Duke asked permission to have him up in his carriage at the races the other day; and, by the Eternal, Sir, he gives the style to all the flunkeys in town!'

'And, I see, he dresses the character,' observed Paul.

'His own idea—entirely. And, by Jove! he proves to be right. You can't do anything here without a uniform. And they tell me he's got everything correct, down to the crest on the buttons.'

They walked on in silence for a few moments, Pendleton retaining a certain rigidity of step and bearing which Paul had come to recognise as indicating some uneasiness or mental disturbance on his part. Hathaway had no intention of precipitating the confidence of his companion. Perhaps experience had told him it would come soon enough. So he spoke carelessly of himself. How the need of a year's relaxation and change had brought him abroad, his journeyings, and, finally, how he had been advised by his German physician to spend a few weeks at Strudle Bad preparatory to the voyage home. Yet he was perfectly aware that the Colonel from time to time cast a furtive glance at his face. 'And *you*,' he said in conclusion—'when do you intend to return to California?'

The Colonel hesitated slightly. "I shall remain in Europe until Miss Arguello is—settled—I mean,' he added hurriedly, 'until she has—ahem!—completed her education in foreign ways and customs. You see, Hathaway, I have constituted myself, after a certain fashion, I may say—still, her guardian. I am an old man, with neither kith nor kin myself, Sir—I'm a little too old-fashioned for the boys over there'—with a vague gesture towards the West, which, however, told Paul how near it still was to him. 'But then, among the old fogeys here—blank it all!—it isn't noticed. So I look after her, you see, or rather make myself responsible for her generally—although, of course, she has other friends and associates, you understand, more of her own age and tastes.'

'And I've no doubt she's perfectly satisfied,' said Paul, in a tone of conviction.

'Well, yes, Sir, I presume so,' said the Colonel, slowly; 'but I've sometimes thought, Mr. Hathaway, that it would have been better if she'd have had a woman's care—the protection, you understand, of an elderly woman of society. That seems to be the style here, you know—a chaperon, they call it. Now, Milly Woods, you see, is about the same age, and the Doña Anna, of course, is older, but—blank it!—she's as big a flirt as the rest—I mean,' he added, correcting himself sharply, 'she lacks balance, Sir, and—what shall I call it?—self-abnegation.'

'Then Doña Anna is still of your party?' asked Paul.

'She is, Sir, and her brother, Don Cæsar. I have thought it advisable, on Yerba's account, to keep up as much as possible the suggestion of her Spanish relationship—although, by reason of their absurd ignorance of geography and political divisions out here, there is a prevailing impression that she is a South American. A fact, Sir. I have myself been mistaken for the Dictator of one of those infernal Republics, and I have been pointed out as ruling over a million or two of niggers like George!"

There was no trace of any conception of humour in the Colonel's face, although he uttered a short laugh, as if in polite acceptance of the possibility that Paul might have one.

Far from that, his companion, looking at the striking profile and erect figure at his side—at the long white moustache which drooped from his dark cheeks, and remembering his own sensations at first seeing George—thought the popular belief not so wonderful. He was even forced to admit that the perfect unconsciousness on the part of master and man of any incongruity or peculiarity in themselves assisted the public misconception. And it was, I fear, with a feeling of wicked delight that, on entering the hotel, he hailed the evident consternation of those correct fellow-countrymen from whom he had lately fled, at what they apparently regarded as a national scandal. He overheard their hurried assurance to their English friends that his companions were *not* from Boston, and enjoyed their mortification that this explanation did not seem to detract from the interest and relief with which the Britons surveyed them, or the open admiration of the Germans.

Although Pendleton somewhat unbent during supper, he did not allude to the secret of Yerba's parentage, nor of any tardy confidence of hers. To all appearance the situation remained as it was three years ago. He spoke of her great popularity as an heiress and a beautiful woman, and the marked attentions she received. He doubted not that she had rejected very distinguished offers, but she kept that to herself. She was perfectly competent to do so. She was no giddy girl, to be flattered or deceived: on the contrary, he had never known a cooler or more sensible woman. She knew her own worth. When she met the man who satisfied her ambition and understanding, she would marry, and not before. He did not know what that ambition was : it was something exalted, of course. He could only say, of his own knowledge, that last year, when they were on the Italian lakes, there was a certain Prince—Mr. Hathaway would understand why he did not mention names—who was not only attentive to her, but attentive to *him*, Sir, by Jove! and most significant in his inquiries. It was the only occasion when he, the Colonel, had ever spoken to her on such subjects ; and, knowing that she was not indifferent to the fellow, who was not bad of his kind, he had asked her why she had not encouraged his suit. She had said, with a laugh, that he couldn't marry her unless he gave up his claim of succession to a certain reigning house; and she wouldn't accept him *without it.* Those were her words, Sir, and he could only say that the Prince left a few days afterwards, and they had never seen him since. As to the Princelings and Counts and Barons, she knew to a day the date of their patents of nobility, and what privileges they were entitled to: she could tell to a dot the value of their estates, the amount of their debts, and, by Jove! Sir, the amount of mortgages she was expected to pay off before she married them. She knew the amount of income she had to bring to the Prussian Army, from the General to the Lieutenant. She understood her own value and her rights. There was a young English Lordling she met on the Rhine, whose boyish ways and simplicity seemed to please her. They were great friends; but he wanted him—the Colonel—to induce her to accept an invitation for both to visit his mother's home in England, that his people might see her. But she declined, Sir! She declined to pass in review before his mother. She said it was for *him* to pass in review before *her* mother.

'Did she say that?' interrupted Paul, fixing his bright eyes upon the Colonel.

'If she had one, Sir, if she had one,' corrected the Colonel, hastily. 'Of course it was only an illustration. That she is an orphan is generally known, Sir.'

There was a dead silence for a few moments. The Colonel leant back in his chair and pulled his moustache. Paul turned away his eyes, and seemed absorbed in reflection. After a moment the Colonel coughed, pushed aside his glass, and, leaning across the table, said, 'I have a favour to ask of you, Mr. Hathaway.'

There was such a singular change in the tone of his voice, an unexpected relaxation of some artificial tension—a relaxation which struck Paul so pathetically as being as much physical as mental, as if he had suddenly been overtaken in some exertion by the weakness of age—that he looked up quickly. Certainly, although still erect and lightly grasping his moustache, the Colonel looked older.

'By all means, my dear Colonel,' said Paul, warmly.

'During the time you remain here you can hardly help meeting Miss Arguello, perhaps frequently. It would be strange if you did not: it would appear to everybody still stranger. Give me your word as a gentleman that you will not make the least allusion to her of the past—nor reopen the subject.'

Paul looked fixedly at the Colonel. 'I certainly had no intention of doing so,' he said after a pause, 'for I thought it was already settled by you beyond disturbance or discussion. But do I understand you, that *she* has shown any uneasiness regarding it? From what you have just told me of her plans and ambition, I can scarcely imagine that she has any suspicion of the real facts.'

'Certainly not,' said the Colonel, hurriedly. 'But I have your promise.'

'I promise you,' said Paul, after a pause, 'that I shall neither introduce nor refer to the subject myself, and that if *she* should question me again regarding it, which is hardly possible I will reveal nothing without your consent.'

'Thank you,' said Pendleton, without, however, exhibiting much relief in his face. 'She will return here to-morrow.'

'I thought you said she was absent for some days,' said Paul.

'Yes; but she is coming back to say good-bye to Doña Anna, who arrives here with her brother the same day, on their way to Paris.'

It flashed through Paul's mind that the last time he had seen her was in the company of the Briones. It was not a pleasant coincidence. Yet he was not aware that it had affected him, until he saw the Colonel watching him.

'I believe you don't fancy the brother,' said Pendleton.

For an instant Paul was strongly tempted to avow his old vague suspicions of Don Cæsar, but the utter hopelessness of reopening the whole subject again, and his recollection of the passage in Pendleton's letter that purported to be Yerba's own theory of his dislike, checked him in time. He only said, 'I don't remember whether I had any cause for disliking Don Cæsar; I can tell better when I see him again,' and changed the subject. A few moments later the Colonel summoned George from some lower region of the hotel, and rose to take his leave. 'Miss Arguello, with her maid and courier, will occupy her old suite of rooms here,' he remarked, with a return of his old imperiousness. 'George has given the orders for her. *I* shall not change my present lodgings, but, of course, will call every day. Good night!'

CHAPTER VI

THE next morning Paul could not help noticing an increased and even exaggerated respect paid him by the hotel attendants. He was asked if his *Excellency* would be served with breakfast in a private room, and his condescension in selecting the public coffee-room struck the obsequious chamberlain, but did not prevent him from preceding Paul backwards to the table, and summoning a waiter to attend specially upon ' milor.' Surmising that George and the Colonel might be in some way connected with this extravagance, he postponed an investigation till he should have seen them again.

And, although he hardly dared to confess it to himself, the unexpected prospect of meeting Yerba again fully preoccupied his thoughts. He had believed that he would eventually see her in Europe, in some vague and indefinite way and hour: it had been in his mind when he started from California. That it would be so soon, and in such a simple and natural manner, he had never conceived.

He had returned from his morning walk to the *Brunnen*, and was sitting idly in his room, when there was a knock at the door. It opened to a servant bearing a salver with a card. Paul lifted it with a slight tremor, not at the engraved name of 'Maria Concepcion de Arguellos de la Yerba Buena,' but at the remembered schoolgirl hand that had pencilled underneath the words 'wishes the favour of an audience with his Excellency the Lord Lieutenant Governor of the Californias.'

Paul looked inquiringly at the servant. 'The *gnädige Fräulein* was in her own salon. Would *Excellency* walk that way? It was but a step; in effect, the next apartment.'

Paul followed him into the hall with wondering steps. The door of the next room was open, and disclosed a handsomely furnished salon. A tall graceful figure rose quickly from behind a writing-table, and advanced with outstretched hands and a frank yet mischievous smile. It was Yerba.

Standing there in a greyish hat, mantle, and travelling dress, all of one subdued yet alluring tone, she looked as beautiful as when he had last seen her—and yet—unlike. For a brief bitter moment his instincts revolted at this familiar yielding up in his fair countrywomen of all that was distinctively original in them to alien tastes and habits, and he resented the plastic yet characterless mobility which made Yerba's Parisian dress and European manner fit her so charmingly and yet express so little. For a brief critical moment he remembered the placid, unchanging simplicity of German and the inflexible and ingrained reserve of English girlhood, in opposition to this indistinctive cosmopolitan grace. But only for a moment. As soon as she spoke, a certain flavour of individuality seemed to return to her speech.

'Confess,' she said, 'it was a courageous

thing for me to do. You might have been somebody else—a real Excellency—or Heaven knows what! Or, what is worse, in your new magnificence you might have forgotten one of your oldest, most humble, but faithful subjects.' She drew back and made him a mock ceremonious curtsey, that even in its charming exaggeration suggested to Paul, however, that she had already made it somewhere seriously.

'But what does it all mean?' he asked, smiling, feeling not only his doubts and uneasiness vanish, but even the years of separation melt away in her presence. 'I know I went to bed last night a very humble individual, and yet I seem to awaken this morning a very exalted personage. Am I really Commander of the Faithful, or am I dreaming? Might I trouble you, as my predecessor Abou Hassan did Sweetlips, to bite my little finger?'

'Do you mean to say you have not seen the *Anzeiger*?' she returned, taking a small German printed sheet from the table and pointing to a paragraph. Paul took the paper. Certainly there was the plain announcement among the arrivals of 'His Excellency Paul

Hathaway, Lord Lieutenant Governor of the Californias.' A light flashed upon him.

'This is George's work. He and Colonel Pendleton were here with me last night.'

'Then you have seen the Colonel already?' she said, with a scarcely perceptible alteration of expression, which, however, struck Paul.

'Yes. I met him at the theatre last evening.' He was about to plunge into an animated description of the Colonel's indignation, but checked himself, he knew not why. But he was thankful the next moment that he had.

'That accounts for everything,' she said, lifting her pretty shoulders with a slight shrug of weariness. 'I had to put a stop to George's talking about *me* three months ago—his extravagance is something *too* awful. And the Colonel, who is completely in his hands—trusting him for everything, even the language —doesn't see it.'

'But he is extravagant in the praise of his friends only, and you certainly justify all he can say.'

She was taking off her hat, and stopped for a moment to look at him thoughtfully, with the soft tendrils of her hair clinging to her forehead. 'Did the Colonel talk much about me?'

'A great deal. In fact, I think we talked of nothing else. He has told me of your triumphs and your victims; of your various campaigns and your conquests. And yet I dare say he has not told me all—and I am dying to hear more.'

She had laid down her hat and unloosed a large bow of her mantle, but stopped suddenly in the midst of it and sat down again. 'I wish you'd do something for me.'

'You have only to name it.'

'Well, drop all this kind of talk! Try to think of me as if I had just come from California—or, better, as if you had never known anything of me at all—and we met for the first time. You could, I dare say, make yourself very agreeable to such a young lady who was willing to be pleased—why not to me? I venture to say you have not ever troubled yourself about me since we last met. No—hear me through—why, then, should you wish to talk over what didn't concern you at the time?

Promise me you will stop this reminiscent gossip, and I promise you *I* will not only not

Crossed her knees with her hands clasped over them

bore you with it, but take care that it is not intruded upon you by others. Make yourself pleasant to me by talking about yourself and your prospects—anything but *me*—and I will throw over those Princes and Barons that the Colonel has raved about and devote myself to you while you are here. Does that suit your Excellency?' She had crossed her knees, and, with her hands clasped over them, and the toe of her small boot advanced behind her skirt, leaned forward in the attitude he remembered to have seen her take in the summer-house at Rosario.

'Perfectly,' he said.

'How long will you be here?'

'About three weeks: that, I believe, is the time allotted for my cure.'

'Are you really ill,' she said quietly, 'or imagine yourself so?'

'It amounts to about the same thing. But my cure may not take so long,' he added, fixing his bright eyes upon her.

She returned his gaze thoughtfully, and they remained looking at each other silently.

'Then you are stronger than you give yourself credit for. That is very often the case,' she said quietly. 'There,' she added in another tone, 'it is settled. You will come and go as you like, using this salon as your own. Stay, we can do something to-day. What do you say to a ride in the forest this afternoon? Milly isn't here yet, but it will be quite proper for you to accompany me on horseback, though, of course, we couldn't walk a hundred yards down the *Allée* together unless we were *verlobt*.'

'But,' said Paul, 'you are expecting company this afternoon. Don Cæsar—I mean, Miss Briones and her brother are coming here to say good-bye.'

She regarded him curiously, but without emotion.

'Colonel Pendleton should have added that they were to remain here overnight as my guests,' she said composedly. 'And, of course, we shall be back in time for dinner. But that is nothing to you. You have only to be ready at three o'clock. I will see that the horses are ordered. I often ride here, and the people know my tastes and habits. We will have a pleasant ride and a good long talk together, and I'll show you a ruin and a distant view of the villa where I have been staying.' She held out her hand with a frank girlish smile, and even a girlish anticipation of pleasure in her brown eyes. He bent over her slim fingers for a moment, and withdrew.

When he was in his own room again, he was conscious only of a strong desire to avoid the Colonel until after his ride with Yerba. He would keep his word so far as to abstain from allusion to her family or her past: indeed, he had his own opinion of its futility. But it would be strange if, with his past experience, he could not find some other way to determine her convictions or win her confidence during those two hours of companionship. He would accept her terms fairly; if she had any ulterior design in her advances, he would detect it; if she had the least concern for him, she could not continue long an artificial friendship. But he must not think of that!

By absenting himself from the hotel he managed to keep clear of Pendleton until the hour arrived. He was gratified to find Yerba in the simplest and most sensible of habits, as if she had already divined his tastes and had wished to avoid attracting undue attention. Nevertheless, it very prettily accentuated her tall graceful figure, and Paul, albeit, like most artistic admirers of the sex, not recognising a

Both rode well and naturally

woman on a horse as a particularly harmonious spectacle, was forced to admire her. Both rode well and naturally—having been brought up in the same Western school—the horses recognised it, and instinctively obeyed them, and their conversation had the easy deliberation and inflection of a *tête-à-tête*. Paul, in view of her previous hint, talked to her of himself and his fortunes—of which she appeared, however, to have some knowledge. His health had obliged him lately to abandon politics and office; he had been successful in some ventures, and had become a junior partner in a bank with foreign correspondence. She listened to him for some time with interest and attention, but at last her face became abstracted and thoughtful. 'I wish I were a man!' she said suddenly.

Paul looked at her quickly. For the first time he detected in the ring of her voice something of the passionate quality he fancied he had always seen in her face.

'Except that it might give you better control of your horse, I don't see why,' said Paul. 'And I don't entirely believe you.'

'Why?'

'Because no woman really wishes to be a man unless she is conscious of her failure as a woman.'

'And how do you know I'm not?' she said, checking her horse and looking in his face. A quick conviction that she was on the point of some confession sprang into his mind, but unfortunately showed in his face. She beat back his eager look with a short laugh. 'There, don't speak, and don't look like that. That remark was worthy the usual artless maiden's invitation to a compliment, wasn't it? Let us keep to the subject of yourself. Why, with your political influence, don't you get yourself appointed to some diplomatic position over here?'

'There are none in our service. You wouldn't want me to sink myself in some absurd social functions, which are called by that name, merely to become the envy and hatred of a few rich Republicans, like your friends who haunt foreign Courts?'

'That's not a pretty speech—but I suppose I invited *that* too. Don't apologise. I'd rather see you flare out like that than pay compliments. Yet I fancy you're a diplomatist, for all that.'

'You did me the honour to believe I was

one once, when I was simply the most palpable ass and bungler living,' said Paul, bitterly.

She was still sweetly silent, apparently preoccupied in smoothing out the mane of her walking horse. 'Did I?' she said softly. He drew close beside her.

'How different the vegetation is here from what it is with us!' she said with nervous quickness, directing his attention to the grass road beneath them, without lifting her eyes. 'I don't mean what is cultivated—for I suppose it takes centuries to make the lawns they have in England—but even here the blades of grass seem to press closer together, at if they were crowded or overpopulated, like the country; and this forest, which has been always wild and was a hunting park, has a *blasé* look, as if it was already tired of the unchanging traditions and monotony around it. I think over there Nature affects and influences us: here, I fancy, it is itself affected by the people.'

'I think a good deal of Nature comes over from America for that purpose,' he said drily.

And I think you are breaking your promise

—besides being a goose!' she retorted smartly. Nevertheless, for some occult reason they both seemed relieved by this exquisite witticism, and trotted on amicably together. When Paul lifted his eyes to hers he could see that they were suffused with a tender mischief, as of a reproving yet secretly admiring sister, and her strangely delicate complexion had taken on itself that faint Alpine glow that was more of an illumination than a colour. 'There,' she said gaily, pointing with her whip as the wood opened upon a glade through which the parted trees showed a long blue curvature of distant hills, 'you see that white thing lying like a snowdrift on the hills?'

'Or the family washing on a hedge.'

'As you please. Well, that is the villa.'

'And you were very happy there?' said Paul, watching her girlishly animated face.

'Yes; and as you don't ask questions, I'll tell you why. There is one of the sweetest old ladies there that I ever met—the perfection of old-time courtliness with all the motherishness of a German woman. She was very kind to me, and, as she had no daughter of her own, I

think she treated me as if I was one. At least,
I can imagine how one would feel to her, and
what a woman like that could make of any girl.
You laugh, Mr. Hathaway, you don't understand—but you don't know what an advantage
it would be to a girl to have a mother like that,
and know that she could fall back on her and
hold her own against anybody. She's equipped
from the start, instead of being handicapped.
It's all very well to talk about the value of
money. It can give you every thing but one
thing—the power to do without it.'

'I think its purchasing value would include
even the *gnädige Frau*,' said Paul, who had
laughed only to hide the uneasiness that Yerba's
approach to the tabooed subject had revived in
him. She shook her head; then, recovering
her tone of gentle banter, said : ' There—I've
made a confession. If the Colonel talks to
you again about my conquests, you will know
that at present my affections are centred on the
Baron's mother. I admit it's a strong point in
his—in *anybody's*—favour, who can show an
unblemished maternal pedigree. What a pity
it is you are an orphan, like myself, Mr. Hath·

away! For I fancy your mother must have been a very perfect woman. A great deal of her tact and propriety has descended to you. Only it would have been nicer if she had given it to you, like pocket money, as occasion required—which you might have shared with me—than leaving it to you in one thumping legacy.'

It was impossible to tell how far the playfulness of her brown eyes suggested any ulterior meaning, for, as Paul again drew eagerly towards her, she sent her horse into a rapid canter before him. When he was at her side again, she said: 'There is still the ruin to see on our way home. It is just off here to the right. But if you wish to go over it we shall have to dismount at the foot of the slope and walk up. It hasn't any story or legend that I know of; I looked over the guide-book to cram for it before you came—but there was nothing. So you can invent what you like.'

They dismounted at the beginning of a gentle acclivity, where an ancient waggon-road, now grass-grown, rose smooth as a glacis. Tying their horses to two moplike bushes, they climbed the slope hand in hand like children. There were a few winding broken steps, part of a fallen archway, a few feet of vaulted corridor,

Tying their horses to two bushes

a sudden breach—the sky beyond—and that was all! Not all—for before them, overlooked at first, lay a chasm covering half an acre, in which the whole of the original edifice—tower turrets, walls, and battlements—had been apparently cast, inextricably mixed and mingled at different depths and angles, with here and there, like mushrooms from a dustheap, a score of trees upspringing.

'This is not Time—but gunpowder,' said Paul, leaning over a parapet of the wall and gazing at the abyss, with a slight grimace.

'It don't look very romantic, certainly,' said Yerba. 'I only saw it from the road before. I'm dreadfully sorry,' she added, with mock penitence. 'I suppose, however, *something* must have happened here.'

'There may have been nobody in the house at the time,' said Paul, gravely. 'The family may have been at the baths.'

They stood close together, their elbows resting upon the broken wall, and almost touching. Beyond the abyss and darker forest they could see the more vivid green and regular lines of the plane-trees of Strudle Bad, the glitter of a spire, or the flash of a dome. From the abyss itself arose a cool odour of moist green leaves, the scent of some unseen blossoms, and around the baking vines on the hot wall the hum of apparently taskless and disappointed bees. There was nobody in sight in the forest road, no one working in the bordering fields,

Their elbows rested upon the broken wall

and no suggestion of the present. There might have been three or four centuries between them and Strudle Bad.

'The legend of this place,' said Paul, glancing at the long brown lashes and oval outline of the cheek so near his own, 'is simple, yet affecting. A cruel, remorseless, but fascinating Hexie was once loved by a simple shepherd. He had never dared to syllable his hopeless affection, or claim from her a syllabled —perhaps I should say a one-syllabled—reply. He had followed her from remote lands, dumbly worshipping her, building in his foolish brain an air-castle of happiness, which by reason of her magic power she could always see plainly in his eyes. And one day, beguiling him in the depths of the forest, she led him to a fair-seeming castle, and, bidding him enter its portals, offered to show him a realisation of his dream. But, lo! even as he entered the stately corridor it seemed to crumble away before him, and disclosed a hideous abyss beyond, in which the whole of that goodly palace lay in heaped and tangled ruins—the fitting symbol of his wrecked and shattered hopes.'

She drew back a little way from him, but still holding on to the top of the broken wall with one slim gauntleted hand, and swung herself to one side, while she surveyed him with smiling parted lips and conscious eyelids. He promptly covered her hand with his own, but she did not seem to notice it.

'That is not the story,' she said, in a faint voice that even her struggling sauciness could not make steadier. 'The true story is called "The Legend of the Goose Girl of Strudle Bad and the enterprising Gosling." There was once a goose-girl of the plain who tried honestly to drive her geese to market, but one eccentric and wilful gosling—— Mr. Hathaway! Stop—please—I beg you let me go!'

He had caught her in his arms—the one encircling her waist, the other hand still grasping hers. She struggled, half laughing; yielded for a breathless moment as his lips brushed her cheek, and—threw him off. 'There!' she said, 'that will do: the story was not illustrated.'

'But, Yerba,' he said, with passionate eagerness, 'hear me—it is all God's truth—I love you!'

She drew back farther, shaking the dust of the wall from the folds of her habit. Then, with a lower voice and a paler cheek, as if his lips had sent her blood and utterance back to her heart, she said : 'Come, let us go.'

'But not until you've heard me, Yerba.'

'Well, then—I believe you—there!' she said, looking at him.

'You believe me?' he repeated eagerly, attempting to take her hand again.

She drew back still farther. 'Yes,' she said, 'or I shouldn't be here now. There! that must suffice you. And if you wish me still to believe you, you will not speak of this again while we are out together. Come, let us go back to the horses.'

He looked at her with all his soul. She was pale, but composed, and—he could see—determined. He followed her without a word. She accepted his hand to support her again down the slope without embarrassment or reminiscent emotion. The whole scene through which she had just passed might have been buried in the abyss and ruins behind her. As she placed her foot in his hand to remount, and for a moment rested her weight upon his shoulder, her brown eyes met his frankly and without a tremor.

Nor was she content with this. As Paul at first rode on silently, his heart filled with unsatisfied yearning, she rallied him mischievously. Was it kind in him on this, their first day together, to sulk in this fashion? Was it a promise for their future excursions? Did he intend to carry this lugubrious visage through the *Allee* and up to the courtyard of the hotel, to proclaim his sentimental condition to the world? At least, she trusted he would not show it to Milly, who might remember that this was only the *second time* they had met each other. There was something so sweetly reasonable in this, and withal not without a certain hopefulness for the future, to say nothing of the half-mischievous, half-reproachful smile that accompanied it, that Paul exerted himself, and eventually recovered his lost gaiety. When they at last drew up in the courtyard, with the flush of youth and exercise in their faces, Paul felt he was the object of envy to the loungers, and of fresh gossip to Strudle Bad. It struck him less pleasantly that two dark faces, which had been previously regarding him in the gloom of the corridor and vanished as he approached, reappeared some moments later in Yerba's salon as Don Cæsar and Doña Anna, with a benignly different expression. Doña Anna especially greeted him with so much of the ostentatious archness of a confident and forgiving woman to a momentarily recreant lover that he felt absurdly embarrassed in Yerba's presence. He was thinking how he could excuse himself, when he noticed a beautiful basket of flowers on the table and a tiny note bearing a Baron's crest. Yerba had put it aside with—as it seemed to him at the moment—an almost too pronounced indifference—and an indifference that was strongly contrasted to Doña Anna's eagerly expressed enthusiasm over the offering, and her ultimate supplications to Paul and her brother to admire its beauties and the wonderful taste of the donor.

All this seemed so incongruous with Paul's feelings, and above all with the recollection of his scene with Yerba, that he excused himself from dining with the party, alleging an engagement with his old fellow-traveller the German officer, whose acquaintance he had renewed. Yerba did not press him; he even fancied she looked relieved. Colonel Pendleton was coming; Paul was not loth, in his present frame of mind, to dispense with his company. A conviction that the Colonel's counsel was not the best guide

'So I hear you, too, are a conquest of the beautiful South American'

for Yerba, and that in some vague way their interests were antagonistic, had begun to force itself upon him. He had no intention of being disloyal to her old guardian, but he felt that Pendleton had not been frank with him since his return from Rosario. Had he ever been so with *her*? He sometimes doubted his disclaimer.

He was lucky in finding the General disengaged, and together they dined at a restaurant and spent the evening at the *Kursaal*. Later, at the Residenz Club, the General leaned over his beer-glass and smilingly addressed his companion.

'So I hear you, too, are a conquest of the beautiful South American.'

For an instant Paul, recognising only Doña Anna under that epithet, looked puzzled.

'Come, my friend,' said the General, regarding him with some amusement, 'I am an older man than you, yet I hardly think I could have ridden out with such a goddess without becoming her slave.'

Paul felt his face flush in spite of himself. 'Ah! you mean Miss Arguello,' he said hurriedly, his colour increasing at his own mention of that name as if he were imposing it upon his honest companion. 'She is an old acquaintance of mine—from my own State—California.'

'Ah, so,' said the General, lifting his eyebrows in profound apology. 'A thousand pardons.'

'Surely,' said Paul, with a desperate attempt to recover his equanimity, '*you* ought to know our geography better.'

'So, I am wrong. But still the name—Arguello—surely that is not American? Still, they say she has no accent, and does not look like a Mexican.'

For an instant Paul was superstitiously struck with the fatal infelicity of Yerba's selection of a foreign name, that now seemed only to invite that comment and criticism which she should have avoided. Nor could he explain it at length to the General without assisting and accentuating the deception, which he was always hoping in some vague way to bring to an end. He was sorry he had corrected the General; he was furious that he had allowed himself to be confused.

Happily his companion had misinterpreted his annoyance, and with impulsive German friendship threw himself into what he believed to be Paul's feelings. '*Donnerwetter!* Your beautiful countrywoman is made the subject of curiosity just because that stupid Baron is persistent in his serious attentions. That is quite enough, my good friend, to make *Klatschen* here among those animals who do not understand the freedom of an American girl, or that an heiress may have something else to do with her money than to expend it on the Baron's mortgages. But'—he stopped, and his simple, honest face assumed an air of profound and sagacious cunning—' I am glad to talk about it with you, who, of course, are perfectly familiar with the affair. I shall now be able to know what to say. My word, my friend, has some weight here, and I shall use it. And now you shall tell me *who* is our lovely friend, and *who* were her parents and her kindred in her own home. Her associates here, you possibly know, are an impossible Colonel and his never-before-approached valet, with some South American Indian planters, and, I believe, a pork-butcher's daughter. But of *them*—it makes nothing. Tell me of *her* people.'

With his kindly serious face within a few inches of Paul's, and sympathising curiosity beaming from his pince-nez, he obliged the wretched and conscious-stricken Hathaway to respond with a detailed account of Yerba's parentage as projected by herself and indorsed by Colonel Pendleton. He dwelt somewhat particularly on the romantic character of the Trust, hoping to draw the General's attention away from the question of relationship, but he was chagrined to find that the honest warrior evidently confounded the Trust with some eleemosynary institution and sympathetically glossed it over. 'Of course,' he said, 'the Mexican Minister at Berlin would know all about the Arguello family: so there would be no question there.'

Paul was not sorry when the time came to take leave of his friend; but, once again in the clear moonlight and fresh, balmy air of the *Allée*, he forgot the unpleasantness of the interview. He found himself thinking only of his ride with Yerba. Well! he had told her that he loved her. She knew it now, and, although she had forbidden him to speak further, she had not wholly rejected it. It must be her morbid consciousness of the mystery of her birth that withheld a return of her affections—some half-knowledge, perhaps, that she would not divulge, yet that kept her unduly sensitive of accepting his love. He was satisfied there was no entanglement; her heart was virgin. He even dared to hope that she had *always* cared for him. It was for *him* to remove all obstacles—to prevail upon her to leave this place and return to America with him as her husband, the guardian of her good name, and the custodian of her secret. At times the strains of a dreamy German waltz, played in the distance, brought back to him the brief moment that his arm had encircled her waist by the crumbling wall, and his pulses grew languid, only to leap firmer the next moment with more desperate resolve. He would win her, come what may! He could never have been in earnest before: he loathed and hated himself for his previous passive acquiescence to her fate. He had been a weak tool of the Colonel's from the first: he was even now handicapped by a preposterous promise he had given him! Yes, she was right to hesitate—to question his ability to make her happy! He had found her here, surrounded by stupidity and cupidity—to give it no other name—so patent that she was the common gossip, and had offered nothing but a boyish declaration! As he strode into the hotel that night, it was well that he did not meet the unfortunate Colonel on the staircase!

It was very late, although there was still visible a light in Yerba's salon, shining on her balcony, which extended before and included his own window. From time to time he could hear the murmur of voices. It was too late to avail himself of the invitation to join them, even if his frame of mind had permitted it. He was too nervous and excited to go to bed, and, without lighting his candle, he opened the French window that gave upon the balcony, drew a chair in the recess behind the curtain, and gazed upon the night. It was very quiet; the moon was high, the square was sleeping in a trance of chequered shadows, like a gigantic chessboard, with black foreshortened trees for pawns. The click of a cavalry sabre, the sound of a footfall on the pavement of the distant Königsstrasse were distinctly audible;

a far-off railway whistle was startling in its abruptness. In the midst of this calm the opening of the door of the salon, with the sudden uplifting of voices in the hall, told Paul that Yerba's guests were leaving. He heard Doña Anna's arch accents—arch even to Colonel Pendleton's monotonous baritone!—Milly's high, rapid utterances, the suave falsetto of Don Cæsar, and *her* voice, he thought a rifle wearied—the sound of retiring footsteps, and all was still again.

So still that the rhythmic beat of the distant waltz returned to him, with a distinctiveness that he could idly follow. He thought of Rosario and the rose-breath of the open windows with a strange longing, and remembered the half-stifled sweetness of her happy voice rising with it from the verandah. Why had he ever let it pass from him then, and waft its fragrance elsewhere? Why—— What was that?

The slight turning of a latch! The creaking of the French window of the salon, and somebody had slipped softly half out on the balcony. His heart stopped beating. From his position in the recess of his own window, with his back to the partition of the salon, he could see nothing. Yet he did not dare to move. For with the quickened senses of a lover he felt the diffused and perfumed aura of *her* presence, of *her* garments, of *her* flesh flow in upon him through the open window, and possess his whole breathless being! It was *she*! Like him, perhaps, longing to enjoy the perfect night—like him, perhaps, thinking of——

'So you ar-range to get rid of me—ha! lik thees? To tur-rn me off from your heels like a dog who have follow you—but without a word—without a—a—thanks—without a 'ope! Ah!—we have ser-rved you—me and my sister; we are the or-range dry—now we can go! Like the old shoe, we are to be flung away! Good! But I am here again—you see. I shall speak, and you shall hear-r.'

Don Cæsar's voice—alone with her! Paul gripped his chair and sat upright.

'Stop! Stay where you are! How dared you return here?' It was Yerba's voice, on the balcony, low and distinct.

'Shut the window! I shall speak with you what you will not the world to hear.'

'I prefer to keep where I am, since you have crept into this room like a thief.'

'A thief! Good!' He broke out in Spanish, and, as if no longer fearful of being overheard, had evidently drawn nearer the window. 'A thief. Ha! *muy bueno*—but it is not *I*, you understand—I, Cæsar Briones, who am the thief! No! It is that swaggering *espadachin*—that *fanfarron* of a Colonel Pendleton—that pattern of an official, Mr. Hathaway—that most beautiful heiress of the Californias, Miss *Arguello*—that are thieves! Yes —of a *name*—Miss Arguello—of a *name*! The name of Arguello!'

Paul rose to his feet.

'Ah, so! You start—you turn pale—you flash your eyes, Señora, but you think you have deceived me all these years. You think I did not see your game at Rosario—yes, even when that foolish Castro *muchacha* first put that idea in your head. Who furnished you the facts you wanted? I—Mother of God!— *such facts!*—I, who knew the Arguello pedigree

—I, who know it was as impossible for you to be a daughter of them as—what ? let me think —as—as it is impossible for you to be the wife of that Baron whom you would deceive with the rest! Ah, yes; it was a high flight for you, Mees—Mees—Doña Fulana—a noble game for you to bring down!'

Why did she did not speak? What was she doing? If she had but uttered a single word of protest, of angry dismissal, Paul would have flown to her side. It could not be the paralysis of personal fear: the balcony was wide; she could easily pass to the end; she could even see his open window.

'Why did I do this? Because I loved you, Señora—and you knew it! Ah! you can turn your face away now; you can pretend to misunderstand me, as you did a moment ago; you can part from me now like a mere acquaintance— but it was not always so! No, it was *you* who brought me here; your eyes that smiled into mine—and drove home the Colonel's request that I and my sister should accompany you. God! I was weak then! You smile, Señora; you think you have succeeded—you and your

R

pompous Colonel and your clever Governor! You think you have compromised me, and perjured *me*, because of this. You are wrong! You think I dare not speak to this puppet of a Baron, and that I have no proofs. You are wrong!'

'And even if you can produce them, what care I?' said Yerba, unexpectedly, yet in a voice so free from excitement and passion that the weariness which Paul had at first noticed seemed to be the only dominant tone. 'Suppose you prove that I am not an Arguello. Good! You have yet to show that a connection with any of your race would be anything but a disgrace.'

'Ah! you defy me, little one! *Caramba*! Listen, then! You do not know all! When you thought I was only helping you to fabricate your claim to the Arguellos' name, I was finding out *who you really were*! Ah! It was not so difficult as you fondly hope, Señora. We were not all brutes and fools in the early days, though we stood aside to let your people run their vulgar course. It was your hired bully— your respected guardian—this dog of an *espada*-

chin, who let out a hint of the secret—with a prick of his blade—and a scandal. One of my *peon* women was a servant at the convent when you were a child, and recognised the woman who put you there and came to see you as a friend. She overheard the Mother Superior say it was your mother, and saw a necklace that was left for you to wear. Ah! you begin to believe! When I had put this and that together I found that Pepita could not identify you with the child that she had seen. But you, Señora, you *yourself* supplied the missing proof! Yes! you supplied it with the *necklace* that you wore that evening at Rosario, when you wished to do honour to this young Hathaway—the guardian who had always thrown you off! Ah! you now suspect why, perhaps! It was your mother's necklace that you wore, and you said so! That night I sent the good Pepita to identify it; to watch through the window from the garden when you were wearing it; to make it sure as the Creed. I sent her to your room late that night when you had changed your dress that she might examine it among your jewels. And she did—and will swear—look you!—*swear* that it is the one given you as a child by the woman at the convent, who was your mother! And who was that woman—eh? Who was the mother of the Arguello de la Yerba Buena?—who this noble ancestress?'

'Excuse me—but perhaps you are not aware that you are raising your voice in a lady's drawing-room, and that, although you are speaking a language no one here understands, you are disturbing the hotel.'

It was Paul, quiet, pale in the moonlight, erect on the balcony before the window. As Yerba, with a start, retreated quickly into the room, Don Cæsar stepped forward angrily and suspiciously towards the window. He had his hand reached forward towards the handle as if to close the swinging sash against the intruder, when in an instant he was seized by Paul, tightly locked in a desperate grip, and whirled out on the balcony. Before he could gain breath to utter a cry, Hathaway had passed his right arm around the Mexican's throat, effectively stopping his utterance, and, with a supreme effort of strength, dragged him along the wall, falling with him into the open window of his own room. As he did so, to his inexpressible relief he heard the sash closed and the bolt drawn of the salon window, and regained his feet, collected, quiet, and triumphant.

'I am sorry,' he said, coolly dusting his clothes, 'to have been obliged to change the scene of this discussion so roughly, but you will observe that you can speak more freely *here*, and that any altercation *we* may have in this room will be less likely to attract comment.'

'Assassin!' said Don Cæsar, chokingly, as he struggled to his feet.

'Thank you. Relieve your feelings as much as you like here; in fact, if you would speak a little louder you would oblige me. The guests are beginning to be awake,' continued Paul, with a wicked smile, indicating the noise of an opening door and footsteps in the passage, 'and are now able to locate without difficulty the scene of the disturbance.'

Briones apparently understood his meaning, and the success of his stratagem. 'You think you have saved *her* from disgrace,' he said, with a livid smile, in a lower tone and a desperate attempt to imitate Paul's coolness. 'For the present—ah—yees! perhaps in this hotel and this evening. But you have not stop my mouth for—a—to-morrow—and the whole world, Mr. Hathaway.'

'Well,' said Paul, looking at him critically, 'I don't know about that. Of course, there's the equal chance that you may kill me—but that's a question for to-morrow, too.'

The Mexican cast a quick glance at the door and window. Paul, as if carelessly, changed the key of the former from one pocket to the other, and stepped before the window.

'So this is a plot to murder me. Have a care! You are not in your own brigand California!'

'If you think so, alarm the house They will find us quarrelling, and you will only precipitate matters by receiving the insult that will make you fight—before them.'

'I am r-ready, Sir, when and where you will,' said Briones, with a swaggering air but a shifting, furtive eye. 'Open—a—the door.'

'Pardon me. We will leave this room

together in an hour for the station. We will board the night express that will take us in three hours beyond the frontier, where we can each find a friend.'

'But my affairs here—my sister—I must see her.'

'You shall write a note to her at that table, saying that important business—a despatch—has called you away, and we will leave it with the porter to be delivered *in the morning*. Or—I do not restrict you—you can say what you like, provided she don't get it until we have left.'

'And you make of me a prisoner, Sir?'

'No; a visitor, Don Cæsar—a visitor whose conversation is so interesting that I am forced to detain him to hear more. You can pass the time pleasantly by finishing the story I was obliged to interrupt a moment ago. Do you know this mother of Miss Yerba, of whom you spoke?'

'That's m—my affair.'

'That means you don't know her. If you did, you'ld have had her within call. And, as she is the only person who is able to say that

Miss Yerba is *not* an Arguello, you have been very remiss.'

'Ah, bah! I am not one of your—a—lawyers.'

'No; or you would know that, with no better evidence than you have, you might be sued for slander.'

'Ah! Why does not Miss Yerba sue, then?'

'Because she probably expects that somebody will shoot you.'

'As *you*, for instance?'

'Perhaps.'

'And if you do *not*—eh? you have not stop my mouth, but your own. And if you *do*, you help her to marry the Baron, your rival. You are not wise, friend Hathaway.'

'May I remind you that you have not yet written to your sister, and you may prefer to do it carefully and deliberately?'

Don Cæsar arose with a vindictive glance at Paul, and pulled a chair before the table, as the latter placed pen, ink, and paper before him. 'Take your time,' he added, folding his arms and walking towards the window. 'Say what you like, and don't let my presence restrain you.'

The Mexican began to write furiously, then spasmodically, then slowly and reluctantly. 'I war-r-n you, I shall expose all,' he said suddenly.

'As you please.'

'And shall say that if I disappear, you are my murderer—you understand—my *murderer!*'

'Don't consult me on a question of epithets, but go on.'

Don Cæsar recommenced his writing with a malign smile. There was a sudden sharp rap at the door.

Don Cæsar leaped to his feet, grasped his papers, and rushed to the door; but Paul was before him. 'Who is there?' he demanded.

'Pendleton.'

At the sound of the Colonel's voice Don Cæsar fell back. Paul opened the door, admitted the tall figure of the Colonel, and was about to turn the key again. But Pendleton lifted his hand in grim deprecation.

'That will do,' Mr. Hathaway. 'I know all. But I wish to speak with Briones elsewhere, alone.'

'Excuse me, Colonel Pendleton,' said Paul, firmly, 'but I have the prior claim. Words

'That will do, Mr. Hathaway; I know all'

have passed between this gentleman and myself which we are now on our way to the station and

the frontier to settle. If you are willing to accompany us, I shall give you every opportunity to converse with him alone, and arrange whatever business you may have with him, provided it does not interfere with mine.'

'My business,' said Pendleton, 'is of a personal nature, that will not interfere with any claim of yours that Mr. Briones may choose to admit, but is of a private quality that must be transacted between us now.' His face was pale, and his voice, although steady and self-controlled, had that same strange suggestion of sudden age in it which Paul had before noticed. Whether Don Cæsar detected it, or whether he had some other instinctive appreciation of greater security, Paul could not tell. He seemed to recover his swagger again, as he said—

'I shall hear what Colonel Pendleton has to say first. But I shall hold myself in readiness to meet you afterwards—you shall not fear, Sir!'

Paul remained looking from the one to the other without speaking. It was Don Cæsar who returned his glance boldly and defiantly,

Colonel Pendleton who, with thin white fingers pulling his moustache, evaded it. Then Paul unlocked the door, and said slowly: 'In five minutes I leave this house for the station. I shall wait there until the train arrives. If this gentleman does not join me, I shall be better able to understand all this and take measures accordingly.'

'And I tell to you, Meester Hathaway, Sir,' said Don Cæsar, striking an attitude in the doorway, 'you shall do as *I* please—*Caramba!*—and shall beg——'

'Hold your tongue, Sir—or, by the Eternal——' burst out Pendleton, suddenly, bringing down his thin hand on the Mexican's shoulder. He stopped as suddenly. 'Gentlemen, this is childish. Go, Sir!' to Don Cæsar, pointing with a gaunt white finger into the darkened hall. 'I will follow you. Mr. Hathaway, as an older man, and one who has seen a good deal of foolish altercation, I regret, Sir, deeply regret, to be a witness to this belligerent quality in a law-maker and a public man; and I must deprecate, Sir—deprecate, your demand on that gentleman for what, in the folly of youth, you are pleased to call personal satisfaction.'

Prepared to follow them

As he moved with dignity out of the room, Paul remained blankly staring after him. Was it all a dream?—or was this Colonel Pendleton, the duellist? Had the old man gone crazy, or was he merely acting to veil some wild purpose? His sudden arrival showed that Yerba must have sent for him and told him of Don Cæsar's threats: would he be wild enough to attempt to strangle the man in some remote room or in the darkness of the passage? He stepped softly into the hall: he could still hear the double tread of the two men: they had reached the staircase—they were *descending!* He heard the drowsy accents of the night porter and the swinging of the door—they were in the street!

Wherever they were going, or for what purpose, *he* must be at the station, as he had warned them he would be. He hastily threw a few things into his valise, and prepared to follow them. When he went downstairs he informed the porter that owing to an urgent call of business he should try to catch the through express at three o'clock, but they must retain his room and luggage until they heard from him. He remembered Don Cæsar's letter. Had either of the gentlemen, his friends who had just gone out, left a letter or message? No, Excellency; the gentlemen were talking earnestly—he believed, in the South American language—and had not spoken to him.

He informed the porter that owing to a call of business he should try and catch the express

Perhaps it was this that reminded Paul, as

he crossed the square again, that he had made no preparation for any possible fatal issue to himself in this adventure. *She* would know it, however, and why he had undertaken it. He tried to think that perhaps some interest in himself had prompted her to send the Colonel to him. Yet, mingled with this was an odd sense of a certain ridiculousness in his position: there was the absurdity of his prospective antagonist being even now in confidential consultation with his own friend and ally, whose functions he had usurped, and in whose interests he was about to risk his life. And as he walked away through the silent streets the conviction more than once was forced upon him that he was going to an appointment that would not be kept.

He reached the station some ten minutes before the train was due. Two or three half-drowsy, wrapped-up passengers were already on the platform; but neither Don Cæsar nor Colonel Pendleton was among them. He explored the waiting-rooms and even the half-lit buffet, but with no better success. Telling the *Bahnhof Inspector* that his passage was only contingent upon the arrival of one or two companions, and describing them minutely to prevent mistakes, he began gloomily to pace before the ticket-office. Five minutes passed—the number of passengers did not increase; ten minutes; a distant shriek—the hoarse inquiry of the inspector—had the Herr's companions yet *gekommt?* the sudden glare of a Cyclopean eye in the darkness, the on-gliding of the long-jointed and gleaming-spotted serpent, the train —a hurried glance around the platform, one or two guttural orders, the slamming of doors, the remounting of black-uniformed figures like caryatides along the *marchepieds*, a puff of vapour, and the train had come and gone without them.

Yet he would give his adversary fifteen minutes more to allow for accident or delay, or the possible arrival of the Colonel with an explanation, and recommenced his gloomy pacing, as the *Bahnhof* sank back into half-lit repose. At the end of five minutes there was another shriek. Paul turned quickly to the inspector. Ah, then, there was another train? No; it was only the *up express* for Basle, going the

S

other way and stopping at the *Nord Station,* half a mile away. It would not stop here, but the Herr would see it pass in a few moments at full speed.

It came presently, with a prolonged despairing shriek, out of the darkness; a flash, a rush and roar at his side, a plunge into the darkness again with the same despairing cry; a flutter of something white from one of the windows, like a loosened curtain, that at last seemed to detach itself, and, after a wild attempt to follow, suddenly soared aloft, whirled over and over, dropped, and drifted slowly, slantwise, to the ground.

The inspector had seen it, ran down the line, and picked it up. Then he returned with it to Paul with a look of sympathising concern. It was a lady's handkerchief, evidently some signal waved to the well-born Herr, who was she only passenger on the platform. So, possibly, it might be from his friends, who by some stupid mischance had gone to the wrong station, and — *Gott im Himmel!* — it was hideously stupid, yet possible, got on the wrong train!

The Herr, a little pale, but composed, thought it *was* possible. No; he would not

It was a lady's handkerchief

telegraph to the next station—not yet—he would inquire.

He walked quickly away, reaching the hotel breathlessly, yet in a space that seemed all too brief for his disconnected thought. There were signs of animation in the hall, and an empty carriage was just re-entering the courtyard. The hall-porter met him with demonstrative concern and apology. Ah! if he had only understood his Excellency better, he could have saved him all this trouble. Evidently his Excellency was going with the Arguello party, who had ordered a carriage, doubtless, for the same important journey, an hour before, yet had left only a few moments after his Excellency. And his Excellency, it would appear, had gone to the wrong station.

Paul pushed hurriedly past the man and ascended to his room. Both windows were open, and in the faint moonlight he could see that something white was pinned to his pillow. With nervous fingers he relit his candles, and found it was a note in Yerba's handwriting. As he opened it, a tiny spray of the vine that had grown on the crumbling wall fell at his feet. He picked it up, pressed it to his lips, and read, with dim eyes, as follows :—

'You know now why I spoke to you as I did to-day, and why the other half of this precious spray is the only memory I care to carry with me out of this crumbling ruin of all my hopes. You were right, Paul: my taking you there *was an omen*—not to you, who can never be anything but proud, beloved, and true—but to *me* of all this shame and misery. Thank you for all you have done—for all you would do, my friend, and don't think me ungrateful, only because I am unworthy of it. Try to forgive me, but don't forget me, even if you must hate me. Perhaps, if you knew all—you might still love a little the poor girl to whom you have already given the only name she can ever take from you—YERBA BUENA!'

CHAPTER VII

IT was already autumn, and in the city of New York an early Sunday morning breeze was sweeping up the leaves that had fallen from the regularly planted ailantus trees before the brown-stone frontage of a row of monotonously alike five-storeyed houses on one of the principal avenues. The Pastor of the Third Presbyterian Church, that uplifted its double towers on the corner, stopped before one of these dwellings, ran up the dozen broad steps and rang the bell. He was presently admitted to the sombre richness of a hall and drawing-room with high-backed furniture of dark carved woods, like cathedral stalls, and, hat in hand, somewhat impatiently awaited the arrival of

She was regular and resolute in features

his hostess and parishioner. The door opened to a tall, white-haired woman in lustreless black silk. She was regular and resolute in features, of fine but unbending presence, and, though somewhat past middle age, showed no signs of either the weakness or mellowness of years.

'I am sorry to disturb your Sabbath morning meditations, Sister Argalls, nor would I if it were not in the line of Christian duty; but Sister Robbins is unable to-day to make her usual Sabbath hospital visit, and I thought if you were excused from the Foreign Missionary class and Bible instruction at three you might undertake her functions. I know, my dear old friend,' he continued, with bland deprecation of her hard-set eyes, 'how distasteful this promiscuous mingling with the rough and ungodly has always been to you, and how reluctant you are to be placed in the position of being liable to hear coarse, vulgar, or irreverent speech. I think, too, in our long and pleasant pastoral relations, you have always found me mindful of it. I admit I have sometimes regretted that your late husband had not more generally familiarised you with the ways of the world. But so it is—we all have our weaknesses. If not one thing, another. And as Envy and

Uncharitableness sometimes find their way in even Christian hearts, I should like you to undertake this office for the sake of example. There are some, dear Sister Argalls, who think that the rich widow who is most liberal in the endowment of the goods that Providence has entrusted to her hands claims therefore to be exempt from labour in the Christian vineyard. Let us teach them how unjust they are.'

'I am willing,' said the lady, with a dry, determined air. 'I suppose these patients are not professedly bad characters?'

'By no means. A few, perhaps; but the majority are unfortunates—dependent either upon public charity or some small provision made by their friends.'

'Very well.'

'And you understand that though they have the privilege of rejecting your Christian ministrations, dear Sister Argalls, you are free to judge when you may be patient or importunate with them.'

'I understand.'

The Pastor was not an unkindly man, and,

as he glanced at the uncompromising look in Mrs. Argalls' eyes, felt for a moment some inconsistency between his humane instincts and his Christian duty. 'Some of them may require, and be benefited by, a stern monitress, and Sister Robbins, I fear, was weak,' he said consolingly to himself, as he descended the steps again.

At three o'clock Mrs. Argalls, with a reticule and a few tracts, was at the door of St. John's Hospital. As she displayed her testimonials and announced that she had taken Mrs. Robbins's place, the officials received her respectfully, and gave some instructions to the attendants, which, however, did not stop some individual comments.

'I say, Jim, it doesn't seem the square thing to let that grim old girl loose among them poor convalescents.'

'Well, I don't know: they say she's rich and gives a lot o' money away, but if she tackles that swearing old Kentuckian in No. 3, she'll have her hands full.'

However, the criticism was scarcely fair, for Mrs. Argalls, although moving rigidly

along from bed to bed of the ward, equipped
with a certain formula of phrases, nevertheless

He descended the steps

dropped from time to time some practical
common-sense questions that showed an almost

masculine intuition of the patients' needs and requirements. Nor did she betray any of that over-sensitive shrinking from coarseness which the good Pastor had feared, albeit she was quick to correct its exhibition. The languid men listened to her with half-aggressive, half-amused interest, and some of the satisfaction of taking a bitter but wholesome tonic. It was not until she reached the bed at the farther end of the ward that she seemed to meet with any check.

It was occupied by a haggard man, with a long white moustache and features that seemed wasted by inward struggle and fever. At the first sound of her voice he turned quickly towards her, lifted himself on his elbow, and gazed fixedly in her face.

'Kate Howard—by the Eternal!' he said, in a low voice.

Despite her rigid self-possession the woman started, glanced hurriedly around, and drew nearer to him.

'Pendleton!' she said, in an equally suppressed voice. 'What, in God's name, are you doing here?'

'Dying, I reckon—sooner or later,' he said grimly, 'that's what they do here.'

'Kate Howard—by the Eternal!'

'But—what,' she went on hurriedly, still glancing over her shoulder as if she suspected some trick—'what has brought you to this?'

'*You!*' said the Colonel, dropping back exhaustedly on his pillow. 'You and your daughter.'

'I don't understand you,' she said quickly, yet regarding him with stern rigidity. 'You know perfectly well I have *no* daughter. You know perfectly well that I've kept the word I gave you ten years ago, and that I have been dead to her as she has been to me.'

'I know,' said the Colonel, 'that within the last three months I have paid away my last cent to keep the mouth of an infernal scoundrel shut who *knows* that you are her mother, and threatens to expose her to her friends. I know that I'm dying here of an old wound that I got when I shut the mouth of another hound who was ready to bark at her two years after you disappeared. I know that between you and her I've let my old nigger die of a broken heart, because I couldn't keep him to suffer with me, and I know that I'm here a pauper on the State. I know that, Kate, and when I say it I don't regret it. I've kept my word to *you*, and, by the Eternal, your daughter's worth it! For if there ever was a fair and peerless creature —it's your child!'

'And she—a rich woman—unless she squandered the fortune I gave her—lets you lie here!' said the woman, grimly.

'She don't know it.'

'She *should* know it! Have you quarrelled?' She was looking at him keenly.

'She distrusts me, because she half-suspects the secret, and I hadn't the heart to tell her all.'

'All? What does she know? What does this man know? What has been told her?' she said rapidly.

'She only knows that the name she has taken she has no right to.'

'Right to? Why, it was written on the Trust—Yerba Buena.'

'No, not that. She thought it was a mistake. She took the name of Arguello.'

'What?' said Mrs. Argalls, suddenly grasping the invalid's wrist with both hands. 'What name?' Her eyes were startled from their rigid coldness, her lips were colourless.

'Arguello! It was some foolish school-girl

fancy which that hound helped to foster in her. Why—what's the matter, Kate?'

The woman dropped the helpless man's wrist, then, with an effort, recovered herself sufficiently to rise, and with an air of increased decorum, as if the spiritual character of their interview excluded worldly intrusion, adjusted the screen around his bed, so as partly to hide her own face and Pendleton's. Then, dropping into the chair beside him, she said in her old voice, from which the burden of ten long years seemed to have been lifted—

'Harry, what's that you're playing on me?'

'I don't understand you,' said Pendleton, amazedly.

'Do you mean to say you don't know it, and didn't tell her yourself?' she said curtly.

'What? Tell her what?' he repeated impatiently.

'That Arguello *was* her father!'

'Her father?' He tried to struggle to his elbow again, but she laid her hand masterfully upon his shoulder and forced him back. 'Her father!' he repeated hurriedly. 'José Arguello! Great God!—are you sure?'

Quietly and yet mechanically gathering the scattered tracts from the coverlet, and putting them back one by one in her reticule, she closed it and her lips with a snap as she uttered—
'Yes.'

Pendleton remained staring at her silently. 'Yes,' he muttered, 'it may have been some instinct of the child's, or some diabolical fancy of Briones'. But,' he said bitterly, 'true or not, she has no right to his name.'

'And I say she *has*.'

She had risen to her feet, with her arms folded across her breast, in an attitude of such Puritan composure that the distant spectators might have thought she was delivering an exordium to the prostrate man.

'I met José Arguello, for the second time, in New Orleans,' she said slowly, 'eight years ago. He was still rich, but ruined in health by dissipation. I was tired of my way of life. He proposed that I should marry him to take care of him and legitimatise our child. I was forced to tell him what I had done with her, and that the Trust could not be disturbed until she was of age and her own mistress. He assented.

T

We married, but he died within a year. He died, leaving with me his acknowledgment of her as his child, and the right to claim her if I chose.'

'And?' interrupted the Colonel with sparkling eyes.

'*I don't choose.*'

'Hear me!' she continued firmly. 'With his name and my own mistress, and the girl, as I believed, properly provided for and ignorant of my existence, I saw no necessity for reopening the past. I resolved to lead a new life as his widow. I came north. In the little New England town where I first stopped, the country people contracted my name to Mrs. Argalls. I let it stand so. I came to New York and entered the service of the Lord and the bonds of the Church, Henry Pendleton, as Mrs. Argalls, and have remained so ever since.'

'But you would not object to Yerba knowing that you lived, and rightly bore her father's name?' said Pendleton, eagerly.

The woman looked at him with compressed lips. 'I should. I have buried all my past and all its consequences. Let me not seek to reopen it or recall them.'

'But if you knew that she was as proud as yourself, and that this very uncertainty as to her name and parentage, although she has never known the whole truth, kept her from taking the name and becoming the wife of a man whom she loves?'

'Whom she loves!'

'Yes; one of her guardians—Hathaway—to whom you entrusted her when she was a child.'

'Paul Hathaway—but *he* knew it.'

'Yes. But *she* does not know he does. He has kept the secret faithfully even when she refused him.'

She was silent for a moment, and then said—

'So be it. I consent.'

'And you'll write to her?' said the Colonel eagerly.

'No. But *you* may, and if you want them I will furnish you with such proofs as you may require.'

'Thank you.' He held out his hand with

such a happy, yet childish gratitude upon his worn face that her own trembled slightly as she took it. 'Good-bye!'

'I shall see you soon,' she said.

'I shall be here,' he said grimly.

'I think not,' she returned with the first relaxation of her smileless face, and moved away.

As she passed out she asked to see the house surgeon. How soon did he think the patient she had been conversing with could be removed from the hospital with safety? Did Mrs. Argalls mean 'far'? Mrs. Argalls meant as far as *that*—tendering her card and eminently respectable address. Ah!—perhaps in a week. Not before? Perhaps before, unless complications ensued; the patient had been much run down physically, though, as Mrs. Argalls had probably noticed, he was singularly strong in nervous will force. Mrs. Argalls *had* noticed it, and considered it an extraordinary case of conviction—worthy of the closest watching and care. When he was able to be moved she would send her own carriage and her own physician to superintend his transfer. In the meantime he was to want for nothing. Certainly, he had given very little trouble, and, in

How soon did he think the patient could be removed

fact, wanted very little. Just now he had only asked for paper, pens, and ink.

CHAPTER VIII

AS Mrs. Argalls' carriage rolled into Fifth Avenue, it for a moment narrowly grazed another carriage, loaded with luggage, driving up to an hotel. The abstracted traveller within it was Paul Hathaway, who had returned from Europe that morning.

Paul entered the hotel, and, going to the register mechanically, turned its leaves for the previous arrivals, with the same hopeless patience that had for the last six weeks accompanied this habitual preliminary performance on his arrival at the principal European hotels. For he had lost all trace of Yerba, Pendleton,

Milly, and the Briones from the day of their departure. The entire party seemed to have separated at Basle, and, in that eight-hours start they had of him, to have disappeared to the four cardinal points. He had lingered a few days in London to transact some business; he would linger a few days longer in New York before returning to San Francisco.

The daily papers already contained his name in the list of the steamer passengers who arrived that morning. It might meet *her* eye, although he had been haunted during the voyage by a terrible fancy that she was still in Europe, and had either hidden herself in some obscure provincial town with the half-crazy Pendleton, or had entered a convent, or even, in reckless despair, had accepted the name and title of some penniless nobleman. It was this miserable doubt that had made his homeward journey at times seem like a cruel desertion of her, while at other moments the conviction that Milly's Californian relatives might give him some clue to her whereabouts made him feverishly fearful of delaying an hour on his way to San Francisco. He did not believe that she had tolerated the company of Briones a single moment after the scene at the Bad Hof, and yet he had no confidence in the Colonel's attitude towards the Mexican. Hopeless of the future as her letter seemed, still its naïve and tacit confession of her feelings at the moment was all that sustained him.

Two days passed, and he still lingered aimlessly in New York. In two days more the Panama steamer would sail—yet in his hesitation he had put off securing his passage. He visited the offices of the different European steamer lines, and examined the recent passenger lists, but there was no record of any of the party. What made his quest seem the more hopeless was his belief that, after Briones' revelation, she had cast off the name of Arguello and taken some other. She might even be in New York under that new name now.

On the morning of the third day, among his letters, was one that bore the postmark of a noted suburban settlement of wealthy villa-owners on the Hudson River. It was from Milly Woods, stating that her father had read of his arrival in the papers, and begged he would dine and stay the next night with them at 'Under Cliff,' if he 'still had any interest in

It was from Milly Woods

the fortunes of old friends. Of course,' added the perennially incoherent Milly, 'if it bores you we shan't expect you.' The quick colour came to Paul's careworn cheek. He telegraphed assent, and at sunset that afternoon stepped off the train at a little private woodland station—so abnormally rustic and picturesque in its brown-bark walls covered with scarlet Virginia creepers that it looked like a theatrical erection.

Mr. Woods's station wagon was in waiting, but Paul, handing the driver his valise, and ascertaining the general direction of the house, and that it was not far distant, told him to go on and he would follow afoot. The tremor of vague anticipation had already come upon him; something that he knew not whether he feared or longed for, only that it was inevitable, had begun to possess him. He would soon recover himself in the flaring glory of this woodland, and the invigoration of this hale October air.

It was a beautiful and brilliant sunset, yet not so beautiful and brilliant but that the whole opulent forest around him seemed to challenge and repeat its richest as well as its most delicate dyes. The reddening west, seen through an opening of scarlet maples, was no longer red; the golden glory of the sun, sinking over a promontory of gleaming yellow sumach that jutted out into the noble river, was shorn of its intense radiance; at times in the thickest woods he seemed surrounded by a yellow nimbus; at times so luminous was the glow of these translucent leaves that the position of the sun itself seemed changed, or the shadows cast in defiance of its glory. As he walked on, long reaches of the lordly placid stream at his side were visible, as far as the terraces of the opposite shore, lifted on basaltic columns, themselves streaked and veined with gold and fire. Paul had seen nothing like this since his boyhood; for an instant the great heroics of the Sierran landscape were forgotten in this magnificent harlequinade.

A dim footpath crossed the road in the direction of the house, which for the last few moments had been slowly etching itself as a soft vignette in a tinted aureole of walnut and maple upon the steel blue of the river. He was hesitating whether to take this short cut or continue on by the road, when he heard the rustling of quick footsteps among the fallen leaves of the variegated thicket through which it stole. He stopped short, the leafy screen shivered and parted, and a tall graceful figure, like a draped and hidden Columbine, burst through its painted foliage. It was Yerba!

She ran quickly towards him

She ran quickly towards him, with parted lips, shining eyes, and a few scarlet leaves clinging to the stuff of her worsted dress in a way that recalled the pink petals of Rosario.

'When I saw you were not in the wagon and knew you were walking, I slipped out to intercept you, as I had something to tell you before you saw the others. I thought you wouldn't mind.' She stopped, and suddenly hesitated.

What was this new strange shyness that seemed to droop her eyelids, her proud head, and even the slim hand that had been so impulsively and frankly outstretched towards him? And he—Paul—what was he doing? Where was this passionate outburst that had filled his heart for nights and days? Where this eager tumultuous questioning that his feverish lips had rehearsed hour by hour? Where this desperate courage that would sweep the whole world away if it stood between them? Where, indeed? He was standing only a few feet from her—cold, silent, and tremulous!

She drew back a step, lifted her head with a quick toss that seemed to condense the moisture in her shining eyes, and sent what might have been a glittering dew-drop flying into the loosed tendrils of her hair. Calm and erect again, she put her little hand to her jacket pocket.

'I only wanted you to read a letter I got yesterday,' she said, taking out an envelope.

The spell was broken. Paul caught eagerly at the hand that held the letter, and would have drawn her to him; but she put him aside gravely but sweetly.

'Read that letter!'

'Tell me of *yourself* first!' he broke out passionately. 'Why you fled from me, and why I now find you here, by the merest chance, without a word of summons from yourself, Yerba? Tell me who is with you? Are you free and your own mistress—free to act for yourself and me? Speak, darling—don't be cruel! Since that night I have longed for you, sought for you, and suffered for you every day and hour. Tell me if I find you the same Yerba who wrote '——

'Read that letter!'

'I care for none but the one you left me have read and re-read it, Yerba—carried it always with me. See! I have it here!' He was in the act of withdrawing it from his breast-pocket, when she put up her hand piteously.

'Please, Paul, please—read this letter first!'

There was something in her new supplicating grace, still retaining the faintest suggestion of her old girlish archness, that struck him. He took the letter and opened it. It was from Colonel Pendleton.

Plainly, concisely, and formally, without giving the name of his authority or suggesting his interview with Mrs. Argalls, he had informed Yerba that he had documentary testimony that she was the daughter of the late José de Arguello, and legally entitled to bear his name. A copy of the instructions given to his wife, recognising Yerba Buena, the ward of the San Francisco Trust, as his child and hers, and leaving to the mother the choice of making it known to her and others, was enclosed.

Paul turned an unchanged face upon Yerba, who was watching him eagerly, uneasily, almost breathlessly.

'And you think this concerns *me*!' he said bitterly. 'You think only of this, when I speak of the precious letter that bade me hope, and brought me to you?'

'Paul,' said the girl, with wondering eyes and hesitating lips; 'do you mean to say that —that—this is—nothing to you?'

'Yes—but forgive me, darling!' he broke out again, with a sudden vague remorsefulness, as he once more sought her elusive hand. 'I am a brute—an egotist! I forgot that it might be something to *you*.'

'Paul,' continued the girl, her voice quivering with a strange joy, 'do you say that you—*you* yourself, care nothing for this?'

'Nothing,' he answered, gazing at her transfigured face with admiring wonder.

'And'—more timidly, as a faint aurora kindled in her cheeks—'that you don't care—that—that—I am coming to you *with a name* to give you in—exchange?'

He started.

'Yerba, you are not mocking me? You will be my wife?'

She smiled, yet moving softly backwards with the grave stateliness of a vanishing yet beckoning goddess, until she reached the sumach-bush from which she had emerged. He followed. Another backward step, and it yielded to let her through; but even as it did so she caught him in her arms, and for a single moment it closed upon them both, and hid them in its glory. A still lingering song-bird, possibly convinced that he had mistaken the season, and that spring had really come, flew out with a little cry to carry the message South; but even then Paul and Yerba emerged with such innocent, childlike gravity, and, side by side, walked so composedly towards the house, that he thought better of it.

U

CHAPTER IX

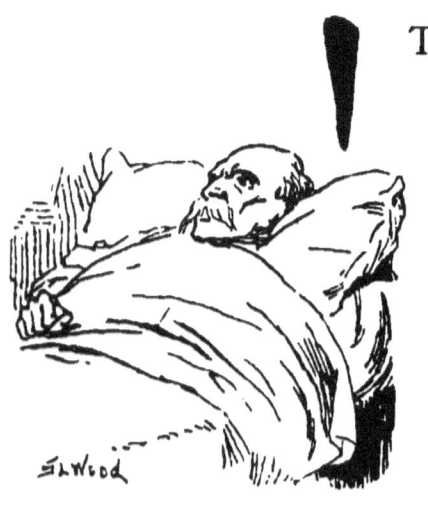

IT was only the *third* time they had ever met—did Paul consider that when he thought her cold? Did he know now why she had not understood him at Rosario? Did he understand now how calculating and selfish he had seemed to her that night? Could he look her in the face now —no, he must be quiet—they were so near the house, and everybody could see them!—and say that he had ever believed her capable of making up that story of the Arguellos? Could he not have guessed that she had some memory of that name in her childish recollections, how or where she knew not? Was it strange that a daughter should have an instinct of her father? Was it kind to her to know all this himself and yet reveal nothing? Because her mother and father had quarrelled, and her mother had run away with somebody and left her a ward to strangers—was that to be concealed from her, and she left without a name? This, and much more, tenderly reproachful, bewildering and sweetly illogical, yet inexpressibly dear to Paul, as they walked on in the gloaming.

More to the purpose, however, the fact that Briones, as far as she knew, did not know her mother, and never before the night at Strudle Bad had ever spoken of her. Still more to the purpose, that he had disappeared after an interview with the Colonel that night, and that she believed always that the Colonel had bought him off. It was not with *her* money. She had sometimes thought that the Colonel and he were in confidence, and that was why she had lately distrusted Pendleton. But she had refused to take the name of Arguello again after that scene, and had called herself only by the name he had given her—would he forgive her for ever speaking of it as she had?—Yerba Buena. But on shipboard, at Milly's suggestion, and to keep away from Briones, her name had appeared on the passenger list as Miss Good, and they had come, not to New York, but Boston.

It was possible that the Colonel had extracted the information he sent her *from* Briones. They had parted from Pendleton in London, as he was grumpy and queer, and, as Milly thought, becoming very miserly and avaricious as he grew older, for he was always quarrelling over the hotel bills. But he had Mrs. Woods's New York address at Under Cliff, and, of course, guessed where she was. There was no address on his letter: he had said he would write again.

Thus much until they reached the steps of the verandah, and Milly, flying down, was ostentatiously overwhelmed with the unexpected appearance of Mr. Paul Hathaway and Yerba, whom she had been watching from the window for the last ten minutes. Then the appearance of Mr. Woods, Californian and reminiscent, and Mrs. Woods, metropolitan, languid, and forgetful, and the sudden and formal retirement of the girls. An arch and indefinable mystery in the air whenever Paul

Mr. Woods, Californian and reminiscent

and Yerba appeared together—of which even the servants were discreetly conscious.

At dinner Mr. Woods again became retrospective and Californian, and dwelt upon the changes he had noticed. It appeared the old pioneers had in few cases attained a comfortable fortune for their old age. 'I know,' he added, 'that your friend Colonel Pendleton has dropped a good deal of money over in Europe. Somebody told me that he actually was reduced to take a steerage passage home. It looks as if he might gamble—it's an old Californian complaint.' As Paul, who had become suddenly grave again, did not speak, Mrs. Woods reminded them that she had always doubted the Colonel's moral principles. Old as he was, he had never got over that freedom of life and social opinion which he had imbibed in early days. For her part, she was very glad that he had not returned from Europe with the girls, though, of course, the presence of Don Cæsar and his sister during their European sojourn was a corrective. As Paul's face grew darker during this languid criticism, Yerba, who had been watching it with a new and absorbing sympathy, seized the first moment when they left the table to interrogate him with heartbreaking eyes.

'You don't think, Paul, that the Colonel is really poor?'

'God only knows,' said Paul. 'I tremble to think how that scoundrel may have bled him.'

'And all for me! Paul, dear, you know you were saying in the woods that you would never, never touch my money. What'—exultingly—'if we gave it to him?'

What answer Paul made did not transpire, for it seemed to have been indicated by an interval of profound silence.

But the next morning, as he and Mr. Woods were closeted in the library, Yerba broke in upon them with a pathetic face and a telegram in her hand. 'Oh, Paul—Mr. Hathaway—*it's true*!'

Paul seized the telegram quickly: it had no signature, only the line: 'Colonel Pendleton is dangerously ill at St. John's Hospital.'

'I must go at once,' said Paul, rising.

'Oh, Paul'—imploringly—'let me go with you! I should never forgive myself if—*and it's addressed to me*, and what would he think if I didn't come?'

Paul hesitated. 'Mrs. Woods will let Milly go with us—and she can stay at the hotel. 'Say yes,' she continued, seeking his eyes eagerly.

He consented, and in half an hour they were in the train for New York. Leaving Milly at the hotel, ostensibly in deference to the Woods's prejudices, but really to save the presence of a third party at this meeting, Paul drove with Yerba rapidly to the hospital. They were admitted to an anteroom. The house surgeon received them respectfully, but doubtingly. The patient was a little better this morning, but very weak. There was a lady now with him—a member of a religious and charitable guild, who had taken the greatest interest in him—indeed, she had wished to take him to her own home—but he had declined at first, and now he was too weak to be removed.

'But I received this telegram: it must have been sent at his request,' protested Yerba.

The house surgeon looked at the beautiful face. He was mortal. He would see if the patient was able to stand another interview: possibly the regular visitor might withdraw.

When he had gone, an attendant volunteered the information that the old gentleman was perhaps a little excited at times. He was a wonderful man; he had seen a great deal; he talked much of California and the early days; he was very interesting. Ah, it would be all right now if the doctor found him well enough, for the lady was already going—that was she coming through the hall.

She came slowly towards them—erect, grey, grim—a still handsome apparition. Paul started. To his horror, Yerba ran impulsively forward, and said eagerly: 'Is he better? Can he see us now?'

The woman halted an instant, seemed to gather the prayer-book and reticule she was carrying closer to her breast, but was otherwise unchanged. Replying to Paul rather than the young girl, she said rigidly, 'The patient is able to see Mr. Hathaway and Miss Yerba Buena,' and passed slowly on. But as she reached the door she unloosed her black mourning veil from her bonnet, and seemed to drop it across her face with a gesture that Paul remembered she had used twelve years ago.

'She frightens me!' said Yerba, turning a suddenly startled face on Paul. 'Oh, Paul, I

'She frightens me!' said Yerba

hope it isn't an omen, but she looked like someone from the grave!'

'Hush!' said Paul, turning away a face that

was whiter than her own. 'They are coming now.'

The house surgeon had returned a trifle graver. They might see him now, but they must be warned that he wandered at times a little; and, if he might suggest, if it was anything of family importance, they had better make the most of their time and his lucid intervals. Perhaps, if they were old friends—*very* old friends—he would recognise them. He was wandering much in the past—always in the past.

They found him in the end of the ward, but so carefully protected and partitioned off by screens that the space around his cot had all the privacy and security of an apartment. He was very much changed; they would scarcely have known him but for the delicately curved aquiline profile and the long white moustache—now so faint and etherealised as to seem a mere spirit wing that rested on his pillow. To their surprise he opened his eyes with a smile of perfect recognition, and, with thin fingers beyond the coverlid, beckoned to them to approach. Yet there was still a shadow of his old reserve in his reception of Paul, and, although one hand interlocked the fingers of Yerba—who had at

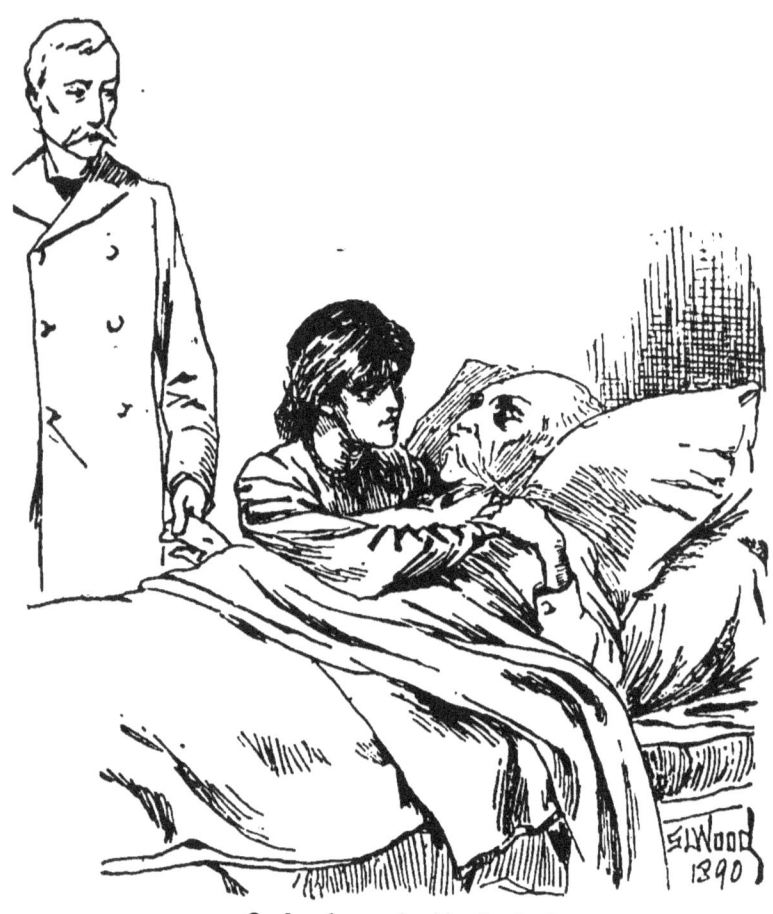

On her knees beside the bed

first rushed impulsively forward and fallen on her knees beside the bed—and the other softly placed itself upon her head, his eyes were fixed upon the young man's with the ceremoniousness due to a stranger.

'I am glad to see, Sir,' he began in a slow, broken, but perfectly audible voice, 'that now you are—satisfied with the right—of this young lady—to bear the name of—Arguello—and her relationship—Sir—to one of the oldest'——

'But, my dear old friend,' broke out Paul, earnestly, 'I *never* cared for that—I beg you to believe'——

'He never—never—cared for it—dear, dear Colonel,' sobbed Yerba, passionately: 'it was all my fault—he thought only of me—you wrong him!'

'*I* think otherwise,' said the Colonel, with grim and relentless deliberation. 'I have a vivid—impression—Sir—of an—interview I had with you—at the St. Charles—where you said'—— He was silent for a moment, and then in a quite different voice called faintly—

'George!'

Paul and Yerba glanced quickly at each other.

'George, set out some refreshment for the Honourable Paul Hathaway. The best, Sir—

you understand. ... A good nigger, Sir—a good boy; and he never leaves me, Sir. Only, by gad! Sir, he will starve himself and his family to be with me. I brought him with me to California away back in the fall of 'forty-nine. Those were the early days, Sir—the early days.'

His head had fallen back quite easily on the pillow now; but a slight film seemed to be closing over his dark eyes, like the inner lid of an eagle when it gazes upon the sun.

'They were the old days, Sir—the days of Men—when a man's *word* was enough for anything, and his trigger-finger settled any doubt. When the Trust that he took from Man, Woman, or Child was never broken. When the tide, Sir, that swept through the Golden Gate came up as far as Montgomery-street.'

He did not speak again. But they who stood beside him knew that the tide had once more come up to Montgomery-street, and was carrying Harry Pendleton away with it.

www.ingramcontent.com/pod-product-compliance
Lightning Source LLC
Chambersburg PA
CBHW022106230426
43672CB00008B/1300